A series of student texts in

CONTEMPORARY BIOLOGY

General Editors:
Professor E. J. W. Barrington, F.R.S.
Dr. Arthur J. Willis

To all those who have encouraged
me in the study of botany

Plant Anatomy:
Experiment and Interpretation

Part I

CELLS AND TISSUES

Elizabeth G. Cutter

B.Sc., Ph.D., D.Sc.

Professor of Botany, University of California, Davis

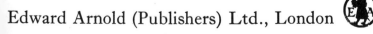

Edward Arnold (Publishers) Ltd., London

First published 1969

Boards Edition SBN: 7131 2216 1
Paper Edition   SBN: 7131 2217 X

Printed in Great Britain by
William Clowes and Sons, Limited, London and Beccles

Preface

This book represents an attempt to relate the structure of plants to the processes of growth and metabolism occurring within them. Plant anatomy is sometimes regarded as a rather static subject, unrelated to the more dynamic aspects of physiology and biochemistry. However, the aim of the plant anatomist or morphologist should surely be not merely to give an accurate description of the organs and tissues that he observes—though that in itself is no mean task—but also to attempt a scientific explanation of how they come into being. Thus the anatomist must seek to discover the factors that control the differentiation and development of the various organs and tissues, and to do so he must relate the structure of the plant to the various processes involved in its growth. The anatomical structure of a plant is best regarded as a visible expression of its genetical complement and physiological processes—a kind of semi-permanent record of the dynamic processes of growth and development that have gone on in the plant and in its various tissues. Unfortunately, our ability to interpret plant structure in these terms is not yet great, and much work remains to be done.

Historically, the study of plant anatomy has involved careful observation of the various organs and tissues of different species of plants, followed by attempts to interpret what was observed. This classical comparative technique has varied little, from the days of the first primitive microscope up to the era of the electron microscope and other complex instruments of the present day, and it has contributed much to our knowledge of plants. In more recent times, greater attention has been paid to developmental aspects of anatomy, and observations have been less restricted to mature material. On the basis of these comparative and developmental observations various hypotheses have been put forward, especially pertaining to the relationships between the structure and function of various parts of the plant. Yet until recently the second part of the scientific method, the devising of experiments which test the validity of the hypotheses propounded on the basis of observation, and finally the interpretation of these experiments, has been only rarely applied to the study of plant anatomy. Such an experimental approach, now becoming more prevalent, is rewarding and strengthens the link between structure and metabolism. However, not all aspects of plant anatomy have so far been treated experimentally. In the chapters which follow I have attempted to provide a basic account of the tissues of flowering plants, with a discussion of relevant experimental results where these exist; I have also endeavoured to relate plant structure to growth processes in the plant wherever possible. Part 2 of this book, to be published later, will deal in a similar way with the aggregations of these tissues that form the organs of the plant. The book follows the orthodox plan of text-books in plant anatomy to a considerable extent, and acknowledgement should be made to other books (see Further Reading), notably those of Esau and Foster, both for this basic plan and for much basic information. The present book differs from others principally in that, where possible, particular emphasis is laid on evidence obtained from modern experimental studies, and this is integrated with existing knowledge of plant structure. The many gaps in our present knowledge are also pointed out and suggestions for possible new investigations are put forward, in an endeavour to stimulate interest in a dynamic and rapidly developing field of botany. Indeed, it will become evident not only that there is scope for much further work of this kind, but also that some of the basic tenets of classical plant anatomy would bear critical re-examination using both analytical and modern experimental techniques.

I am grateful to many authors, including Drs. D. W. Bierhorst, J. Cronshaw, R. E. Dengler, K. Esau, D. A. Fisher, W. A. Jensen, N. J. Lang, K. Mühlethaler, K. D. Stewart, W. S. Walker and R. H. Wetmore, for supplying illustrations previously published by them, and to these and several others, and their publishers, for permission to reproduce illustrations from their publications. These sources are fully acknowledged in the legends to the figures. I am also indebted to Miss Sonia Cook for her skill in making several of the sections from which original illustrations were prepared. A number of friends and colleagues, notably Dr. E. M. Gifford, Jr. and Dr. C. R. Stocking, have read parts of the text and made many valuable suggestions. Dr. Bryan Truelove has read all of the text, over a considerable period, and I am indebted to him not only for the time which he has devoted to this task but for the many constructive criticisms which he has made. I remain solely responsible, however, for all omissions and errors.

I am especially grateful to Dr. A. J. Willis, general editor of this series, not only for his careful reading and criticism of the text, but for his seemingly endless patience, and for that of my publishers. My mother has also been very helpful and has exercised great forbearance during the preparation of this book. But perhaps my most constant, and overwhelming, debt is to those who have taught me botany and in this and other ways have shaped my thought and outlook on botanical matters over the years.

Davis,   E.G.C.
1968.

Acknowledgements

I am indebted to the following publishers and scientific journals for permission to reproduce the figures indicated:

Academic Press, Inc. (Figs. 2.2, 3.7, 4.5, 4.6, 4.8, 4.11, 7.5, 7.12, Table 9.1, Fig. 9.5); Agricultural Publications, University of California (Fig. 9.4); American Journal of Botany (Figs. 2.1a, 3.10, 5.1, 5.4, 6.1g, 6.2, 6.5, 6.6, 7.3, 7.4, 8.3, 8.6, 8.9, 8.12, 10.6); Annual Reviews Inc. (Fig. 3.3); Arnold Arboretum, Harvard University (Figs. 6.1b, 8.10, 8.11); W. H. Freeman and Company (Fig. 3.4); Longmans, Green and Co. Ltd. (Fig. 4.3); New Phytologist (Fig. 11.5); Rockefeller University Press (Figs. 9.3, 9.6, 9.7, 9.8); Scientific American (Figs. 3.4, 9.9); Springer-Verlag (Figs. 2.3, 7.10, 9.1); Syracuse University Press (Fig. 4.10); University of Chicago Press (Fig. 8.7).

Table of Contents

I

Introduction: The Growing Plant

The majority of vascular plants consist of a number of different organs—usually root, stem, leaf and flower—and each of these in turn is made up of a number of different tissues. This complex structure, the whole growing plant, is derived during development from a single cell, the fertilized egg or zygote. Many complex processes of differentiation (see Chapter 2) take place during the ontogeny of the plant.

Usually the zygote divides in such a manner that a filamentous structure is formed. The first, unequal division of the zygote in higher plants results in the formation of a larger cell, which gives rise to the suspensor, and a smaller one which undergoes further division to become the embryo proper. Processes of cellular differentiation ensue, with the result that some cells of the small embryo develop differently from others. The cotyledons (two in dicotyledons, one in monocotyledons and several in gymnosperms, apart from occasional exceptions) may become evident at an early stage (Fig. 1.1a). Eventually meristematic regions, where the cells continue to divide actively for a long period of time, become delineated at each end of the embryo by the progressive vacuolation of the intervening cells. These meristematic areas are the *apical meristems* of the root and shoot, and during growth these important regions of the plant become progressively more distant from one another as a result of their own activity, the rest of the plant being differentiated between them (Figs. 1.1b, 1.2). Polarity is established in the very early stages of embryonic development, probably in the zygote, and this soon becomes manifest by the demarcation of a root end and a shoot end in the young embryo. This establishment of polarity, presumably as a result of physiological changes, is a critical aspect of

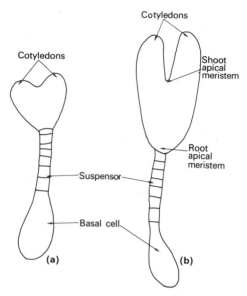

Fig. 1.1 Developing embryos of *Capsella*. (a) Two cotyledons are formed. (b) The apical meristems of the shoot and root are readily distinguishable. × 150.

differentiation and indeed of development in general, and will be discussed further in the next chapter.

The apical meristems of the root and shoot, established at each end of the young embryo, are extremely important regions in the plant, since they remain 'perennially embryonic' and by their activity give rise to all the tissues of the root and the shoot respectively. This type of 'open growth' from an apical meristem is peculiar to plants, and nothing like it is known in animals. Meristematic cells are usually considered to be thin-walled, often relatively rich in cytoplasm and with only small vacuoles, and capable of continued active division. Usually they stain more densely than adjacent more extensively vacuolated cells.

The organs and tissues formed by the activity of these apical meristems constitute the primary plant body (see Esau[91]), and this is composed of primary *tissues*. These are made up of cells, the units of the plant body, each tissue being composed of a restricted range of cell types; in many tissues only one type of cell is present. The three main systems of tissues in the plant may be called the dermal, vascular and ground systems.[91] The dermal system comprises the outer covering layer, the epidermis, during primary growth. The vascular system is made up of the phloem and the xylem, the conducting elements of the plant, which during primary growth

Fig. 1.2 Longitudinal section of fully developed embryo of *Clarkia rubicunda* subsp. *rubicunda*, showing the two cotyledons (c) and the axis between the shoot apex (sa) and radicle apex (ra). The forerunners of the dermal (d), vascular (v) and ground (g) tissue systems are indicated. (By courtesy of Dr. R. E Dengler.) ×180.

develop from the procambium, and the ground tissue includes those tissues distinct from the dermal and vascular components. The ground tissue is often composed of thin-walled parenchyma cells, but more thick-walled strengthening elements, collenchyma and sclerenchyma, may also be present. These various tissues are described in more detail in subsequent chapters.

The tissues are arranged differently in the various **organs** of which the plant is composed. The structure of organs is discussed in detail in Part 2 of this work.[71] The vascular elements often form a rod or cylinder, with ground tissue peripheral, and sometimes also central, to them, and dermal tissue on the periphery. The ground tissue between the dermal and vascular components is commonly called cortex; that within the vascular cylinder, pith. In the root there is often no pith. In the stem the vascular tissue most frequently consists of numerous separate strands, the vascular bundles, but this is not always so; it may also form a cylinder or be arranged in some other way. In the leaf, the vascular system usually forms a network of strands embedded in the ground tissue. In leaves the ground tissue is called mesophyll, and is usually composed of thin-walled cells which contain chloroplasts and function in photosynthesis.

During the ontogeny of most dicotyledons and gymnosperms, and a few monocotyledons, secondary growth occurs. By the activity of special meristems, secondary tissues are formed, which add to the girth of the primary plant body. These meristems are the vascular cambium, which gives rise to secondary xylem and phloem (the secondary conducting tissues), and the phellogen or cork cambium, which gives rise to the periderm, an outer covering which may replace the epidermis when this is ruptured due to the expansion in girth which occurs during secondary growth. The vascular cambium and phellogen are sometimes called *lateral meristems*, on account of their position, to distinguish them from apical meristems. Detailed discussion of apical meristems is deferred to Part 2, when they are considered along with the organs to which they give rise.

The lateral organs of the shoot are formed by the apical meristem. This gives rise to the leaf primordia, meristematic mounds of tissue which eventually develop into leaves. Bud primordia, which usually occur in the axils of leaves, are generally also formed by the shoot apex, but may sometimes dedifferentiate from already more or less mature tissues.

Lateral roots are not formed at the apex of the root, but at some distance away from it. Usually they develop from primordia formed in the pericycle, the outermost layer of the vascular cylinder.

The flower or inflorescence is formed either from the terminal shoot apex or from lateral shoot apices, as a consequence of changes that take place in these regions as a result of certain factors such as daylength.

While an accurate description of the various tissues and organs of the plant is undoubtedly essential, in order to gain a deeper understanding of the reasons underlying the observed structure it is often necessary to carry out experiments and interpret the results. Descriptions of plant structure have been available since the days of Nehemiah Grew [125] and other seventeenth century botanists—though since then they have been improved in many ways with modern methods—but the experimental approach to anatomy is, for the most part, relatively recent. An attempt is made here to integrate the results of experiments, where available, with the results already obtained by careful observation both with the light and electron microscopes. Where appropriate, new approaches to various problems, using experimental methods, have been suggested.

TERMINOLOGY

Certain terms referring to planes of cell division and the direction in which tissues differentiate will be used in the following chapters. These terms, some of which are illustrated in Fig. 1.3, are as follows:

Proximal —situated near or towards the point of attachment of an organ.

Distal —situated away from the point of attachment.

Basipetal —from the apex towards the base; for example, differentiation may occur basipetally.

Acropetal —from the base towards the apex.

Anticlinal —used to describe a cell wall formed at right angles to the surface of the organ. This is an anticlinal wall.

Periclinal —used to describe a cell wall formed parallel to the surface of the organ.

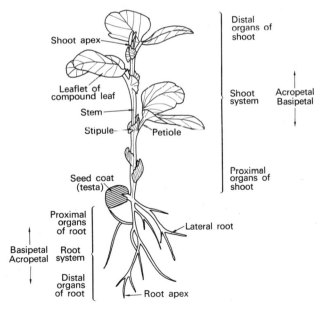

Fig. 1.3 Young plant of *Vicia faba* showing the various organs and illustrating the meaning of certain terms. × 1/3.

2

Differentiation

During the development of a whole plant from a single cell, the fertilized egg or zygote, various processes of differentiation must take place. By repeated division of the zygote and its immediate products, a group of initially fairly homogeneous meristematic cells is formed. By processes of differentiation cells become recognizably different both from the cells which have given rise to them and from neighbouring cells having the same origin as themselves. All this involves complex biochemical and biophysical processes that we are only beginning to understand. It is sometimes said, indeed, that differentiation is one of the most complex unsolved problems of biology. While it is relatively easy to describe the visible manifestation of differentiation, it is much more difficult to explain the underlying causes in terms of the biochemical changes taking place in the cells. It is important to remember that invisible biochemical changes always precede the visible morphological ones; anatomical features may be said to mirror in visible form the less obvious physiological events that took place some time before.

The differentiation of the organs and tissues of the plant is not random, but in fact takes place in a very orderly fashion, according to the species. The control of organization, or orderly development, in plants is as yet little understood, and poses many fascinating and difficult problems. Planes of cell division have formerly been considered to be very important in the control both of the position and of the shape of the developing organ, but recent work with irradiated wheat seedlings suggests that leaves, for example, may develop their characteristic shape despite the prevention of nuclear division by irradiation of the seeds.[127,128] Irradiation of wheat seeds prevented the synthesis of deoxyribonucleic acid (DNA) and stopped mitosis, but did not prevent germination and growth of the seedlings. Such seedlings, designated 'gamma plantlets', thus afford material in which some development takes place in the absence of cell division. However, this growth, interesting as it is, merely involves an expansion of the primordia already present in the embryo, and it seems likely that mitoses which have taken place during embryogenesis may already have determined the shape and polarization of the organs present. This is not to deny, however, that cell enlargement may play a greater role in the determination or development of organ shape than has been attributed to it hitherto. These same workers have recently shown that within the roots of irradiated seedlings cells of the pericycle enlarged but did not divide, giving rise to structures the initial form and position of which resembled those of lateral root primordia.[113]

In the irradiated wheat seedlings tissue differentiation and maturation also took place. Thus the later stages of differentiation, at least, can ensue in the absence of mitosis, but as the authors themselves point out early stages of differentiation had already occurred in the embryo prior to irradiation.[112] This work seems to lay emphasis on the importance of very early phases of development and differentiation in the determination and control of subsequent stages.

Many of the somatic cells of the plant body are often polyploid, and it has sometimes been suggested that the level of ploidy of the cells might control differentiation. However, it seems that in general, at least, polyploidy is merely one manifestation of cell differentiation, rather than a necessary precursor or controlling factor.[199] Thus we must look not to chromosomes, but to the genes themselves, or to factors in the cytoplasm, for the ultimate arbiters of cell and tissue differentiation, at the same time heeding a recent salutary reminder that the genome is itself answerable to external control.[126]

Alternative pathways of development

From numerous experiments both on plants and animals, we know that cells have the capacity to differentiate in many different ways, and that the normal fate of a cell within the organism can be altered. Certain concepts that have been developed by zoologists are useful also in considering cellular differentiation in plants. We may say that in order to respond to stimuli which may influence its differentiation a cell (or organ) must have a certain *competence* to react. It may be capable of following a number of different developmental pathways: some mechanism or stimulus comes into operation which selects one of these pathways, and the fate of the cell is determined. It is thought possible that the attainment of competence may be the synthesis of messengers, the subsequent response to inductive stimuli depending on regulating devices in the cytoplasm.[137] Zoologists have discovered a number of *evocators,* substances which will call forth or evoke a certain type of differentiation in a cell which is competent to respond. Some such substances may also exist in plants, but more probably it is the balance between several substances that is important in differentiation. For example, the balance between the concentrations of auxin and sugar is important in controlling the differentiation of xylem or phloem from tissue which can give rise to either (see Chapter 8).

The potentiality of a cell to differentiate in different ways, and its competence to react to stimuli, may be retained for long periods of time without being manifested. The parenchymatous cells of the pith of the sahuaro cactus (*Cereus giganteus*) may remain in an active state during the 100 or 150 years of the plant's life;[170] furthermore, if an incision is made into the pith, the cells can divide actively and form a cambium-like tissue which gives rise to cork,[201] thus exhibiting a potentiality for differentiation that would not normally have been expressed. As has been aptly pointed out,[252] there must be a system of restraints normally operating within the plant that allows cells to manifest only a small fraction of their actual potentialities for differentiation and development while they remain undisturbed *in situ.*

Polarity

One of the most important factors in early differentiation is the establishment of polarity. This is the setting-up of a difference, structural or physiological, between one end of a cell or organ and the other. Establishment of polarity in the developing zygote, for example, is very important; it may be controlled to some extent by the environment in which the zygote develops. Recent work on the embryo of cotton with the electron microscope[148] demonstrates very clearly the polarized distribution of cytoplasm at the time of early divisions of the zygote (Fig. 2.1).

The importance of environment in establishing polarity has been studied in experiments with fertilized eggs of the brown seaweed *Fucus.* These zygotes develop freely in sea water, i.e. entirely free from a cellular environment, and it is thus possible to impose various single environmental factors upon them. The first visible sign of differentiation in the fertilized egg of *Fucus* is the outgrowth of a rhizoid at one position in the cell wall. The first new cell wall is formed in a plane at right angles to the emerging rhizoid. The factors which determine the position of the rhizoid thus determine the polarity of the developing zygote. Whitaker[277,278] and others have carried out many experiments with *Fucus.* For example, if fertilized eggs of *Fucus* are aggregated together in groups, the rhizoids are formed pointing towards the centre of the group, even if the eggs belong

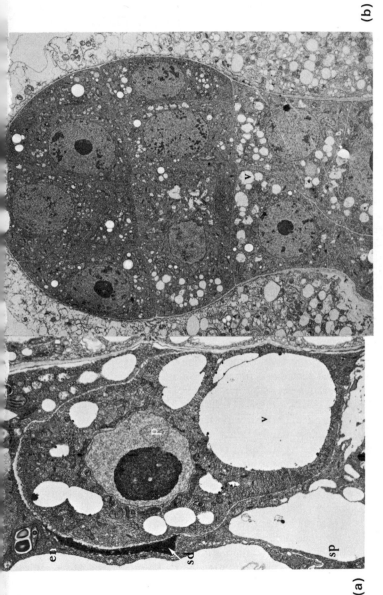

Fig. 2.1 Stages in embryo development showing polarization of the cytoplasm. (a) Zygote of *Capsella bursa-pastoris* soon after fertilization. The cell is already polarized, with a large vacuole (v) at one end and dense cytoplasm at the other. en, endosperm; p, pocket in nucleus, a temporary result of fusion of the egg and sperm nuclei; sd, part of degenerating synergid; sp, persistent synergid. ×4,000. (By courtesy of Sister Richardis Schulz and Dr. W. A. Jensen. From *Am. J. Bot.*, **55**, Fig. 11, p. 813, 1968.) (b) 5-day-old embryo of cotton, *Gossypium hirsutum*. The terminal cells (top) are more densely cytoplasmic and less vacuolate than the cells at the base. v, vacuole. ×2,250. (By courtesy of Dr. W. A. Jensen.)

to different species. It is thought that diffusion gradients of metabolic products are set up. Gradients of temperature and of pH are also effective in determining polarity, rhizoids developing on the more acid side. If *Fucus* zygotes are centrifuged in sea water, stratification of the cytoplasm takes place, and the rhizoid develops at the centrifugal pole.[277] However, if the visible contents of the zygote become redistributed again uniformly after centrifugation but before the formation of rhizoids, these develop at random in relation to the previous stratification. Distribution of the cytoplasm within the cell is thus apparently important. Clearly polarity may be determined, at least to a considerable extent, by external environmental factors. In higher plants the effect of external factors is likely to be less, since the cells in which polarity is becoming established are part of a tissue and may not be in direct contact with the environment. Factors of the internal environment of the plant, however, are clearly important. For example, gradients of various kinds are of some consequence, but the basis of polarity may depend on rather more structural features such as the arrangement of proteins in the outer layers of cytoplasm.[40]

The conjecture that polarity is actually a natural and inevitable consequence of nuclear division has recently been put forward.[38] It is suggested that metabolic conditions at the two ends of a recently formed cell are likely to be different from the outset, as a consequence of disturbance of the cytoplasm at one end by the nuclear spindle. A metabolic gradient could thus be established as a result of cell division, and this could be the basis of polarity. In some instances, however, polarization of the cell seems to precede nuclear division. It has been proposed that 'cellular differentiation may result from the segregation of specific biochemical systems *within* the single parent cell, and that this separation becomes finalized by the laying down of the wall between the two sister cells'.[58] It is often difficult to distinguish between the establishment of polarity and its consequences. Moreover, it is perhaps arguable whether polarity is a factor in the control of differentiation or an early manifestation of it.

Establishment of polarity within a cell may lead to its subsequent unequal division, and to a different fate for the two daughter cells formed by that division. Such unequal or asymmetric divisions are important in the differentiation of various structures.[41] For example, in the formation of many stomata and root hair initials and of some other structures, a cell divides unequally to give two derivatives, a small one with dense cytoplasm, and a larger one with less activity (Fig. 2.2). The small cell differentiates as the guard cell mother cell or root hair initial, the larger one as an ordinary epidermal cell. The visible differentiation of these cells is preceded or accompanied by various differences in enzyme distribution, nucleolar size, etc. (see Chapter 7). It is noteworthy that those structures whose differentiation is preceded by unequal cell divisions of this kind are lacking from

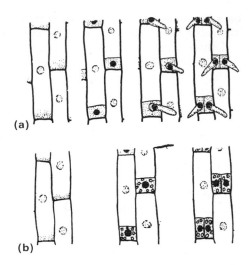

Fig. 2.2 Differentiation of (a) root hairs and (b) stomata in monocotyledons. Successive stages of development are shown from left to right in each figure. Unequal, polarized distribution of cytoplasm is followed by nuclear and cell division resulting in the formation of a large cell and a small one, the latter developing as the root hair or guard cell mother cell. (From Bünning,[40] Fig. 2 (II and III), p. 111.)

gamma plantlets developing after irradiation.[112] Thus asymmetric mitosis does indeed seem to be a factor in their differentiation.

Pattern formation

Differentiated regions or structures, such as root hairs, stomata and procambial strands, are often maintained at some distance from one another, forming a more or less regular pattern. Bünning[40] has applied to these active loci of growth the term *meristemoid*, and has pointed out that they show a degree of mutual incompatibility by means of which the pattern is established and maintained. Meristemoids of a particular kind, e.g. stomata, can inhibit not only other stomata, but also meristemoids with a different destiny, such as hairs. When these regions of active growth become inactive or separated from each other by some distance, new ones can form between them. For example, in the ground tissue of the developing root of *Pandanus* a pattern of cells which will contain raphide (needle-shaped) crystals is found. These cells are initially recognizable by the density of their cytoplasm. After these cells have formed raphides and died, a new pattern of meristemoids is able to form in positions between the raphide cells. These new meristemoids develop as bundles of fibres.[42] In other instances, for example in the differentiation of stomata, the distance between the meristemoids may simply increase as a result of expansion of the organ concerned, this enabling new ones to differentiate in the enlarged spaces between. The differentiation of new stomata in close proximity to existing ones in some species poses a difficulty for this theory.[197]

The nature of the incompatibility which apparently exists between some meristemoids is not yet fully understood. Competition for substances necessary for growth and differentiation could be involved as well as, or instead of, the production of inhibitory substances by the regions of active growth. Whatever its nature, the inhibitory field can apparently extend over an area much greater than that occupied by the meristemoid itself, at least in some instances.

In assessing the importance of the factors involved in differentiation, the effects of one tissue on another should be considered. For example, not only can cells that give rise to hairs affect the differentiation of stomata within a single tissue, the epidermis, by mutual inhibition, but the distribution of the hairs themselves may depend upon the underlying tissues. In the leaf of *Helianthus*, for example, the hair-bearing epidermal cells follow the pattern of the underlying vascular tissue forming the veins (Fig. 2.3a). Again, in the leaf of *Nymphaea alba* the growth and development of the

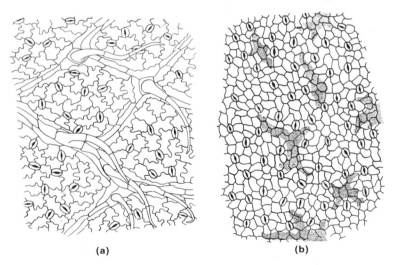

(a)   (b)

Fig. 2.3 Patterns of differentiation. (a) Lower epidermis of the leaf of *Helianthus rigidus*. Hairs are situated over the veins. (b) Leaf of *Nymphaea alba*. The sclereids (stippled) in the mesophyll never occur below stomata. (From Bünning[42], *Handbuch der Pflanzenphysiologie*, **15**, 1, Berlin-Heidelberg-New York: Springer, 1965, Figs. 10 and 11, p. 391.)

sclereids in the mesophyll and the stomata in the epidermis are apparently inter-related, since the sclereids never occur below stomata (Fig. 2.3b).[42] These visible morphological relationships can be readily observed, but the underlying physiological relationships between the various cells and tissues are not yet well understood and some interesting experiments could be designed to study them. For example, incisions could be made in young leaves to separate those tissues that normally differentiate in proximity to each other. Also, the effects of auxin, which has been shown in other species to affect the formation of both stomata and sclereids, might profitably be studied in developing leaves of *Nymphaea*.

The importance of the position of a cell in relation to other tissues is shown also by certain aspects of differentiation in *Monstera deliciosa*, in which unequal cell divisions occur in the cells of various tissue layers. In the epidermis, the small cells give rise to root hairs; in the hypodermis, they differentiate merely as short cells alternating with longer ones, and in the cortex the short cells develop as trichosclereids.[32]

The importance of environment

The example just cited illustrates the importance of the position or environment of a cell in controlling its differentiation. The effects of the external environment are likely to be fairly comparable on all or most of the cells of an organ, but the more immediate environment of a cell may be exceedingly important. As long ago as 1878 Vöchting[263] was emphasizing the importance of the position of a cell in the organism, and later Driesch[79] summed this up for animal development by stating that the fate of a cell is a function of its position. The results of many experiments now convincingly demonstrate that the normal fate of a cell can sometimes be altered by changing environmental factors. This is illustrated, for example, in many every-day horticultural practices. For example, in many species removal of a leaf from the plant will often lead to the formation of roots and a bud from tissues at the base of the leaf that would never have shown any sign of these potentialities if left in their normal environment.

One of the best examples of the importance of environmental factors in controlling differentiation is the recent successful growth of whole plants from isolated cells or small groups of cells, obtained from various tissues of the embryo or adult plant. This possibility has now been demonstrated in a number of species, using cells derived from various tissues and grown under a variety of conditions. Some examples will be briefly discussed.

Steward and his co-workers [251,253] devised a method for growing carrot tissue by excising small discs from the secondary phloem region of carrot roots and placing these in a liquid culture medium, under aseptic conditions. In the presence of coconut milk—the liquid endosperm which nourishes the embryo of the coconut—the phloem tissue began to grow actively, in a manner which it would not have done if left in its normal environment. When explants of carrot tissue were grown in liquid medium with coconut milk in special culture flasks, which were shaken and rotated, some single cells and small groups of cells were loosened from the surface. When these detached cells were grown separately, it was found that only a fairly small proportion of single cells would continue development. Some, however, did grow and developed in a number of ways. Some divided giving rise to filaments of cells which in certain respects resembled normal carrot embryos. These groups of cells eventually formed small roots, and if transferred on to a medium solidified with agar would also form shoots opposite to the root. These 'test-tube' plants could be grown to maturity; indeed, they flowered and produced viable seeds.

If, instead of pieces of phloem, embryos of the wild carrot were caused to proliferate and to separate into free cells, these cells could very readily be induced to develop as embryo-like structures, or *embryoids*, if grown on a medium containing coconut milk.[252] Thus apparently every cell from a young embryo was capable of developing in a manner comparable to that of a normal zygote, if provided with appropriate nutritional conditions. Halperin[131] has also clearly demonstrated the importance of the chemical constitution of the medium in controlling the development of pieces of callus from the petiole of wild carrot as either root-bearing structures or as embryoids. The resemblance of the latter to stages in normal embryogenesis is very striking. Many free cells, e.g. spores of lower plants, seem to give rise to a filamentous type of growth, but the formation of cotyledon-like structures in the carrot embryoids does lead to a truly embryo-like form, although the structures obtained from single cells of some other species do not resemble embryos. These experiments thus indicate that, not only can cells from an embryo behave like zygotes, but so also can mature, fully differentiated cells or their derivatives. The necessary conditions appear to be (i) removal of the cell from its normal environment, and (ii) supplying it with an appropriate chemical environment. The cells must divide actively but be prevented from enlarging.

A fully differentiated carrot cell thus retains the potentialities for growth and differentiation normally manifested only by the zygote, but in its normal environment within the plant exhibits only a few of these potentialities. The limitations on its capacity for development must be imposed by its environment, i.e. by its position within the organism.[251]

The control over the growth and development of a cell exerted by its neighbours must in fact be quite complex, and may possibly change during ontogeny. There is evidence from the experiments with carrot that cells grow better when part of a group than they do in isolation. This is attributed to the action of one or more substances that stimulate cell division, supposedly produced by some of the cells of a group and transmitted to others, probably through the cytoplasmic connections between cells.[28] In such a case, a kind of physiological differentiation would exist in the group of cells, even if no morphological differences between the cells were evident. Perhaps cells that are within a small group are merely less damaged than those that are completely isolated. However, within the whole growing plant, also, actively dividing cells may be stimulated by adjacent less active cells. We are left with the apparent paradox that cells reveal their totipotence only in isolation, not when part of a tissue, which suggests that their normal topographic situation among other cells is acting as a restraint on their development; on the other hand the great majority of cells evidently grow better in association with, or at least in proximity to, other cells which apparently stimulate their growth. This may be one example of the axiom that growth and differentiation are to some extent mutually incompatible.

Genetic control of differentiation

As will by now be apparent, the basic problem of differentiation is that from a population of cells that are initially derived from one cell—the zygote—and are presumably genetically identical, many different tissues become differentiated. It thus appears that differentiation cannot be under direct genetic control. However, although all the cells of the plant may have the same genetic complement not all the genes may be able to express their activity in a cell at any one time. For example, those genes which control floral development presumably do not come into play until the plant has been induced to flower. We may say that during vegetative growth the genes controlling flowering are repressed, becoming active, or derepressed, as the result of appropriate external stimuli, for example exposure to a certain number of hours of alternating darkness and light. Bonner[33] has pointed out that a whole sequence of genetic switching mechanisms may be set in train by an initial induction or trigger. The nature of the agents which can trigger this sequential activation of genes, and the mechanism of their action, are consequently the keys to the control of tissue and organ differentiation. It is known that certain hormonal substances can control gene action, and histones are also important in this respect. It may be noted that, in the zoological terms already described, the evocator might constitute the trigger and the competence of the cell to react could be attributed to its genetic complement and to whether certain genes were repressed or not at that particular time. As Bonner[33] puts it, 'Small molecules, the hormones for example, turn off or on individual or whole sets of genes in appropriate cells of higher organisms eliciting the production of characteristic enzyme molecules and, in appropriate instances, setting a cell or cells on a new pathway of development.' The differential synthesis of enzymes is considered by some[240] to be the basic process of cell differentiation, and certainly it is now known that concentrations of particular enzymes often precede the morphological differentiation of certain cells and tissues.

In later chapters some experimental evidence for the control of differentiation by hormonal substances and for the localization of enzyme systems preceding differentiation is described. However, at least in plants, much work remains to be done to elucidate completely the mechanisms by which these changes are brought about. Clearly, complex interactions between the genetic complement, the biochemistry and the structural features of the whole growing plant are involved.

3

The Plant Cell

Plants, like animals, are composed of cells. Some plants consist of only one cell, but the flowering plants, with which this book is concerned, are made up of many cells which at maturity differ greatly in structure. As we have seen, these differences are the result of processes of differentiation. The cell is the unit of construction of plants, just as atoms are the units of molecules. Recognition of the cellular construction of plants goes back to the seventeenth century, and knowledge of the cell and its contents has progressed hand-in-hand with the development of the microscopes employed for its observation. The advance of biological knowledge is dependent to a considerable extent upon advances in those other disciplines on which biology relies for its tools, for example physics and electronics as well as biochemistry.

In the year 1665 Robert Hooke studied sections of a bottle cork with a microscope which we would now consider extremely primitive. He observed that the cork resembled a honeycomb, consisting of pores that were separated by walls, and he called the individual units *cells*, because of the resemblance to the cells of a honeycomb. Thus at this time attention was largely focused on the cell wall, although botanists were aware that living cells contained liquid contents. Shortly after this, green bodies, the chloroplasts, were observed inside the cells, and in 1833 Robert Brown observed the nucleus, a larger body present in all living cells[147] (with the probable exception of mature sieve elements).

By the middle of the nineteenth century it had been realized that all organisms consist of cells, and, further, that all such units are derived from the division of existing cells. It was shown that chromosomes were present in the nucleus, and that these divided during nuclear division. Nuclear divisions were of two kinds: those that gave rise to the somatic cells of the plant, in which the chromosomes duplicated and the daughter cells had the same number of chromosomes as the original cell (mitosis); and those that gave rise to the reproductive cells of the plant, in which the daughter cells had only half the original number of chromosomes (meiosis).

The cell, then, was known to consist of a cell wall and contents, the protoplasm. This comprised a more or less spherical body, the nucleus, containing chromosomes which were the bearers of the hereditary units or genes, embedded in a granular matrix, the cytoplasm. Various other inclusions were also observed with the light microscope, and biochemical studies led to some understanding of their function. The great expansion in knowledge of cell structure, however, followed the development of the electron microscope, an instrument that employs a beam of electrons instead of a beam of light. This enabled anatomists to observe much smaller structures than are visible with the light microscope, and the study of the fine structure or ultrastructure of plant cells began. Although some valuable work on whole mounts or pieces of cell wall was done earlier, the work on sectioned material dates only from about 1950.

When Robert Hooke observed the cells of the bottle cork, he remarked that he had found 'a new invisible world'. The development of the electron microscope has revealed yet another 'invisible world', one on a much smaller scale. Whereas the upper magnification of the light microscope is about 1,200 times, that of the electron microscope is 160,000 times.[147] With the light microscope—where the lower limit of visibility is determined by the wavelength of light—the smallest objects that could be observed had a diameter of about 0.3μ (micron); with the electron microscope objects of considerably less than 100 Å (Ångströms) can be studied, and the limits of resolution are of the order of 8 or 10 Å (1 mm = 1,000 μ; 1 μ = 10,000 Å). Although electron microscopy has greatly extended our knowledge of plant structure, essentially it is not a new discipline, but merely comparative anatomy on a different scale. When electron microscopy—or, for that matter, classical comparative anatomy—is combined with a biochemical approach, the aim of establishing the function of the various components of the cell can be achieved, at least to some extent. Indeed, investigation of the activities of the cell components on a molecular scale is now possible.

The various components of the plant cell (Fig. 3.1) that are known at the present time will now be listed; each is discussed at more length below. The plant cell is surrounded by a **cell wall** (see Chapter 4), which may be a primary wall only or may comprise both primary and secondary walls; in the wall there may be depressions or pits, and the wall may be traversed by cytoplasmic strands, the **plasmodesmata**. Immediately within the wall the cell contents are delimited by a membrane, the plasma membrane or

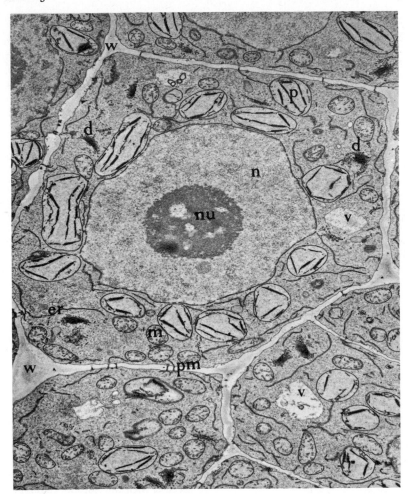

Fig. 3.1 Cell from the ground meristem of the root of *Hydrocharis morsus-ranae* showing the nucleus and various organelles in the cytoplasm. d, dictyosomes; er, endoplasmic reticulum; m, mitochondria; n, nucleus; nu, nucleolus; p, plastids; pm, plasmodesma; v, vacuole; w, cell wall. × c. 14,000. (Photo by Dr. K. D. Stewart.)

plasmalemma; in the cytoplasm there may be one or more *vacuoles*, containing cell sap and each bounded by a membrane, the *tonoplast*. There are also membrane systems, the **endoplasmic reticulum** and the **dictyosomes**. In addition there are a number of organelles, including the **nucleus**, bounded by the nuclear envelope and containing the chromatin and one or more nucleoli; the *plastids*, of which one type, the chloroplasts, are active in photosynthesis; the *mitochondria*, active in respiration; and the *ribosomes*, active in protein synthesis. In some cells substances such as fats and oils, starch, protein bodies and crystals may also be present; these are known as ergastic substances.

Bonner[33] gives an estimate of the approximate numbers of the various organelles that may be present in a plant cell, which may help in visualizing the cell and its continuous activities. He says that the cell contains 'a nucleus (generally one); some chloroplasts, fifty or so . . .; mitochondria, five hundred or so; ribosomes, five hundred thousand or so; and enzyme molecules, five hundred thousand thousand or so.' This emphasizes not only the necessarily extremely small size of these bodies, but also the great physiological activities of various kinds that are going on within each cell.

It is important to remember that cells that we see in illustrations, all those that we observe with the electron microscope, and many of those seen with the light microscope, have been killed, fixed and often also stained. But in life the cell is very different. For in the living cell there is movement of various kinds: Brownian movement; active and often rapid cytoplasmic streaming, effecting the movement of organelles such as plastids and mitochondria; movement of the chromosomes first towards and then away from the spindle; and so on. This movement can be seen in living cells observed with the light microscope, and observations of killed cells with the electron microscope indicate that movement must have occurred.[35,36]

CELL CONTENTS

Endoplasmic reticulum

Within the cytoplasm there is an elaborate system of membranes, the endoplasmic reticulum. This consists of double membranes that enclose spaces or cisternae; these may be more or less cylindrical in shape, or flat and ribbon-like.[237] The membranes of the endoplasmic reticulum, or ER, which are of lipo-protein nature, are connected with the nuclear envelope and also extend to the margins of the cell; connections have also been observed between the ER of adjacent cells.[202] Thus there exists a complicated network of membranes which connects the nucleus of one cell with the cytoplasm and nuclei of adjacent cells. Usually actively growing cells have more ER than resting ones.

The ER is believed to occur in two forms, smooth and rough. The rough form is rendered rough or particulate by the occurrence of numerous small particles of ribonucleoprotein on its outer surface; these ribosomes are involved in protein synthesis. There is continuity between the smooth and rough forms of the ER.

The functions of the ER are not yet well established, and some of those proposed are still controversial. It has been suggested that it forms a transport system for proteins, etc., and that it has a role in wall formation. Northcote[192] states that the ER and the other organelles establish the plane of cell division by the provision and transport of material to be incorporated in the cell plate, by means of the production of vesicles from the cell organelles. He further points out that it has been shown that growth-regulating substances such as auxin and kinetin may affect the plane of cell division, and infers that these substances may influence the organization of the ER during cell division. The plane of cell division, which is linked with the phenomenon of polarity, is usually considered to be of great importance in the fundamental processes of differentiation (see Chapter 2).

Dictyosomes

The Golgi apparatus of plant cells consists of a system of dictyosomes occurring throughout the cytoplasm. A dictyosome consists of a small stack (from 2 to 20) of smooth double membranes enclosing cisternae, which are often dilated at the ends; they are associated at the edges with a number of small vesicles which are thought to have been constricted from them. This is clearly seen in a cross-sectional view of a dictyosome (Figs. 3.1, 3.2). Contrary to former belief, the cisternae comprising the dictyosome are not merely flattened sacs, but have a central region of this kind with, in addition, anastomosing tubular proliferations extending from it. The tubules branch and rejoin to form a complex fenestrated system,[183] the vesicles at the edge being attached to the cisternae by one or more tubules (Fig. 3.3). The number of vesicles seems to vary with cell activity.[276] The number of dictyosomes per cell also varies widely, and in some plant cells may be as many as several thousand.[183]

Dictyosomes are now known to function in secretion (see Chapter 10). Their function in the synthesis and transport of polysaccharides has recently been clearly demonstrated experimentally by combining autoradiography with electron microscopy. Wheat roots were supplied with radioactive glucose and after the material was fixed and sectioned for the electron microscope it was placed in contact with a photographic emulsion sensitive to radioactivity. The point of this technique is that after developing, dark regions are present in the film; these lie over organelles which have incorporated the radioactive substance. By use of this method, labelled material was found in the dictyosomes and associated vesicles, and also in the cell wall. By supplying the radioactive glucose for various short periods of time it could be shown that there was a loss of radioactivity from the dictyosomes with time and an increase in radioactivity in the cell wall, indicating that the product of the dictyosomes was transported there.[193] In the root cap of maize, dictyosomes secreting polysaccharides were charac-

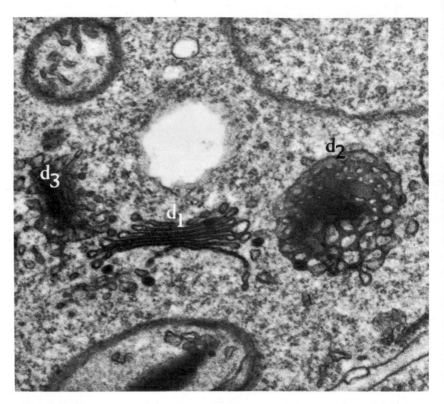

Fig. 3.2 Dictyosomes in a trichoblast of *Hydrocharis morsus-ranae*. d_1, dictyosome in section, showing the stacked cisternae; d_2, section of a dictyosome at right angles to d_1, probably showing a single cisterna (compare Fig. 3.3); d_3, obliquely sectioned dictyosome. × 45,000. (Photo by Dr. K. D. Stewart.)

terized by hypertrophy of the cisternae and the formation of large vesicles.[150,185]

Dictyosomes occur generally in plant cells, and are not restricted to those actively involved in secretion. Vesicles produced by the dictyosomes are incorporated into the cell wall; this other activity of the dictyosomes is particularly evident in root hairs.

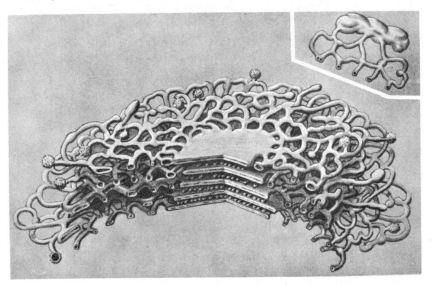

Fig. 3.3 Diagram of part of a dictyosome, composed of five cisternae, from a plant cell. The cisternae are fenestrated, and are separated by intercisternal regions. Vesicles are formed at the edges of the cisternae (see inset). (From Mollenhauer and Morré,[183] Fig. 1, p. 29.)

Microtubules

Small elongated structures, the microtubules, are present in peripheral regions of the cytoplasm, and in some other parts of the cell.[162] The juxtaposition of these structures and the cell wall, and the customary similarity of alignment of the microtubules and the microfibrils in the cell wall, led to the view that the microtubules might be responsible for orientation of cellulose synthesis. However, the observation that in root hairs of radish the axially aligned microtubules were present both where microfibrils were regularly oriented and also in the zone near the tip where microfibrils were randomly oriented suggests that any control that the microtubules may have over wall deposition may be indirect.[191] The recent observation of Halperin and Jensen[132] that microtubules were rarely seen in carrot cells cultured in a medium containing auxin, but became visible parallel to the walls in every cell after removal of auxin, is interesting because of the view that auxin affects wall plasticity. The precise role of the microtubules thus remains to be determined.

Nucleus

In meristematic cells the more or less spherical nucleus occupies a considerable proportion of the volume of the cell, sometimes as much as $\frac{2}{3}$

or $\frac{3}{4}$; this proportion becomes less during differentiation. The nucleus is bounded by a double membrane, the nuclear envelope, which has pores in it at rather regular intervals. The nuclear envelope is connected with the endoplasmic reticulum. Electron-dense chromatic material is present in a ground substance which resembles the cytoplasm but is often of a different density.[276] One or more nucleoli may be present; these are not bounded by membranes. The structure of the chromosomes themselves, the bearers of the genes, is now understood to some extent. The chromosomes consist of nucleoprotein, comprising deoxyribonucleic acid (DNA) and proteins, including histone. The nucleolus, on the other hand, contains ribonucleic acid (RNA) and protein.

The nucleus controls the development of the cell. It is now known that the DNA in the nucleus is capable of controlling the synthesis of a kind of RNA known as messenger RNA. This substance is transported out of the nucleus into the cytoplasm, and there transmits a coded message conveying instructions for the synthesis by the ribosomes of particular proteins. According to which of the genes present in the nucleus are active, or de-repressed (not all of them are functional at any one time in ontogeny), a different kind of messenger RNA will be synthesized, and different proteins will be made; this in turn will affect the development of the cell. The connections which, as we have seen, exist between nucleus and cytoplasm, and between nuclear envelope and ER (and hence ribosomes), are thus seen to be of great importance in the functioning of the nucleus in the control of development.

Ribosomes

Ribosomes are small, more or less spherical organelles which occur free in the cytoplasm, on the outside of the endoplasmic reticulum, and in the nucleus and chloroplasts. The fixative used for many plant cells does not preserve the ribosomes, and thus the ER often appears devoid of these bodies. Ribosomes have a diameter of about 100–150 Å and consist of RNA and protein, mainly histone. They are functionally very important, being the sites of protein synthesis, but as yet no distinctive structure has been ascribed to them. Clusters of ribosomes known as polyribosomes or polysomes may be the actual structures most important in protein synthesis. A striking example in plants are those observed in root hairs of radish.[34]

Mitochondria

These are organelles which lie at about the limits of resolution of the light microscope, but are just visible in the form of small rods or spheres. In the living condition they are selectively stained by Janus Green B. The electron microscope reveals that they are bounded by a double membrane; extensions of the inner membrane form tubular projections into the interior of the organelle. These projections are termed cristae (Fig. 3.4). The mitochondria are concerned with processes of energy conversion, and have been called the powerhouses of the cell. They are the locus of many enzymes in the cell, especially those of the Krebs cycle. Mitochondria are thus concerned with respiration. The origin of mitochondria is by no means

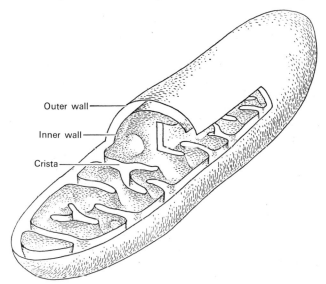

Outer wall

Inner wall

Crista

Fig. 3.4 Diagram of a mitochondrion with part of its double membrane cut away. The cristae are infoldings of the membrane. (From A. L. Lehninger (1961), How cells transform energy. *Scient. Am.*, **205**, Fig. a, p. 72. Copyright © (1961) by Scientific American, Inc. All rights reserved.)

certain, and various workers have claimed that they originate from other components of the cell; but it seems most likely that they originate by fission of existing mitochondria. Mitochondria contain some DNA, and apparently also a small amount of RNA.[25]

Numerous mitochondria occur in each plant cell, whether meristematic or differentiated; glandular cells usually contain a greater number.[119] In some cells, e.g. sieve tube elements, the mitochondria undergo degeneration.

Plastids

Plastids may be divided into two types: pigmented and non-pigmented. Pigmented plastids consist of *chloroplasts*, which are green in colour and in which the pigment chlorophyll predominates, and *chromoplasts*, which are usually yellow, orange or red and contain the pigment carotene. Non-pigmented plastids or leucoplasts include *amyloplasts*, which synthesize starch, *elaioplasts*, which synthesize fats or oils, and some authors include plastids which synthesize storage protein. A comprehensive account of the chemistry, inheritance and structure of plastids has recently been published.[154]

These plastids are all derived from very small bodies, the proplastids, which are present in egg cells and in cells of the apical meristems.[124,270] The development of these bodies into amyloplasts has been followed, for example, in the root cap of maize.[276] The proplastids may undergo fission three or four times. It is considered that leucoplasts and chromoplasts originate by the arrest at particular phases of the normal sequence of development of a chloroplast from a proplastid.[124]

Amyloplasts are usually found in storage organs, such as the potato tuber, and in other deep-seated tissues. They are capable of developing into chloroplasts on exposure to light. Elaioplasts are mainly found in certain monocotyledons. Chromoplasts occur in many flowering parts, e.g. petals and fruits (Fig. 3.5), and also in roots, e.g. carrot. They vary greatly in shape and size, and are often rather angular. They may develop from

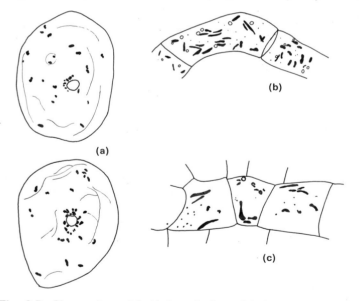

Fig. 3.5 Chromoplasts (black) in cells from (a) fruit of *Cyphomandra*; (b) fruit of *Capsicum*; (c) root of *Daucus* (carrot). (a) ×150. (b) and (c) ×240.

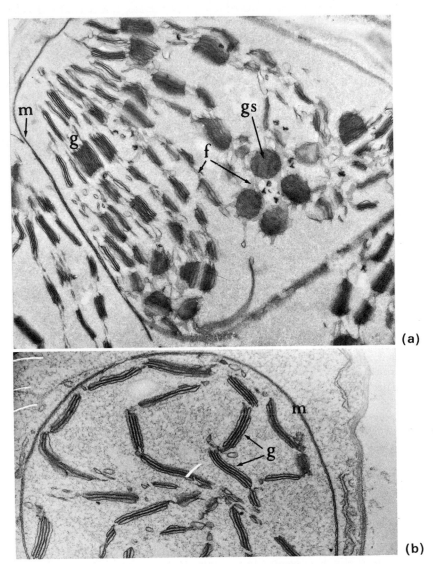

Fig. 3.6 Plastids of *Lemna minor*. (a) Parts of two adjacent plastids. The grana are seen both in side and surface view. ×14,200. (b) Part of a younger plastid showing grana composed of only a few lamellae. ×19,500. f, frets; g, grana in side view; gs, grana in surface view; m, plastid membrane. (By courtesy of Dr. Norma Lang.)

chloroplasts, e.g. in the fruits of orange or tomato, but may also develop directly from proplastids.

Chloroplasts occur principally in leaves and the cortex of young stems, in parenchymatous or collenchymatous tissues exposed to the light. They are concerned with energy reactions in the cell, with photosynthesis and the build-up of temporary starch. In addition to chlorophyll and other pigments they contain protein and RNA, and—at least in certain species— some DNA. Recent results suggest a close relationship between protein metabolism in the leaf and the photosynthetic activities of the chloro-plasts.[205] There are usually several chloroplasts in each cell; according to one estimate there are 403,000 chloroplasts in each square millimetre of the leaf of the castor bean, *Ricinus communis*.[124] As has been pointed out, movement of various kinds occurs within plant cells, and the chloroplasts possess a degree of mobility. For example, in many plants light intensity affects the orientation of the chloroplasts; at low light intensity the broad surface of the plastid faces the light, and at high intensities the edge of the plastid faces the light, indicating some movement of the organelles.

Chloroplasts appear more or less homogeneous or slightly granular under the light microscope, but with the electron microscope they are seen to have a complex structure. They are bounded by a double semi-permeable mem-brane, within which is a colourless matrix, or *stroma*, which often con-tains starch grains. Within the stroma there are several *grana*, each of which is composed of a series of double-membrane lamellae, or thylakoids, stacked one upon the other like a pile of discs or pennies (Fig. 3.6a, b). The grana are interconnected by a system of intergranal lamellae, or frets, that pass through the stroma (Fig. 3.6a).[124,269] Several grana are present in each chloroplast; the chloroplasts of tobacco, for example, each have 40–80 grana.[124] Recent work on cultured callus tissue obtained from tobacco pith showed that the grana in chloroplasts of light-grown callus cells had only 4–7 lamellae. However, chloroplasts from non-growing callus cells ap-proaching senescence had grana comparable with those in mature leaves.[158]

Chloroplasts develop from proplastids by flattened vesicles budding off from the inner membrane of the proplastid. These increase in number and form collapsed double-membrane lamellae, which are aggregated in rows in some areas to give rise to the grana and become green. If barley seed-lings are grown in the dark, the rate of fusion of vesicles is slow and instead they accumulate to form a structure known as the prolamellar body. If left in the dark for three to ten days a 'crystal lattice' structure is developed; this may give rise eventually to concentric lamellae if the seedlings are maintained in darkness (Fig. 3.7).[124] In proplastids from tobacco callus grown in the dark, however, a prolamellar body was not observed. In the dark the lamellae did not fuse to form grana as they did in the light.[158] More work is needed on the effects of light on plastid development.

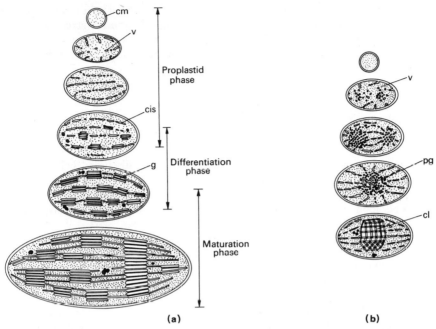

Fig. 3.7 Stages in the development of a proplastid into a chloroplast. **(a)** In the light. **(b)** In the dark showing the development of the prolamellar body (pg) and crystal lattice (cl). cm, double membrane of the chloroplast; v, vesicle; cis, flattened cisterna; g, granum. (From Granick,[124] Fig. 25, p. 535. Modified after von Wettstein.)

It is evident that many cells that do not normally form chloroplasts retain the ability to do so. For example, plants derived from single phloem cells, or small groups of cells, of the carrot root, which are normally devoid of chloroplasts, and buds derived from epidermal cells of flax stems, in which plastid development is arrested at an early stage, both produce chloroplasts. The question of why plastid development is arrested in the cells of the epidermis, but not in the underlying mesophyll or cortex, poses an interesting developmental problem which has not been investigated.

Weier[270] has discussed the origin of mitochondria and plastids, and has pointed out that if mitochondria and plastids arose from a common precursor organelle in meristematic tissues, for which there is no experimental evidence, then the enzyme systems involved in respiration and photosynthesis must also have had a common precursor. If there was such a common precursor for the enzyme systems it must be of great antiquity and have occurred in simple organisms the descendants of which in fact have no organized organelles. Others[119] consider that the system of mitochondria may be phylogenetically derived from that of the plastids. Weier suggests that, in view of the great range in plastid structure in different taxonomic groups, pathways of photosynthesis may vary and may have been a factor in evolution. In contrast, mitochondria from different groups are very similar.

Ergastic substances

Starch

Starch grains, and the other cell inclusions to be discussed below, are formed as a result of metabolic activity in the cell, and are sometimes known as ergastic substances. Some of these are waste products, others are stored food material. Starch grains characteristically stain bluish-black with a solution of iodine in potassium iodide.

The carbohydrate starch is composed of long-chain molecules which are symmetrically spaced and consequently confer some crystalline properties on the starch grains. This can be seen by viewing the grains under polarized light, when they will appear clear and luminous against a black background, as crystals do. A dark cross is visible at the hilum of the starch grain. The hilum is the centre of origin of the grain; around it layers of carbohydrate are deposited. These appear as striations, like contours, in the grain, because of a difference in diffraction between successive layers of starch. This gives the starch grain some superficial resemblance to the shell of a mussel. The hilum may be centrally situated in the grain, or it may be eccentric, as in potato starch (Fig. 3.8a). This contributes to the considerable range of form among starch grains. Compound starch grains with two or more hila

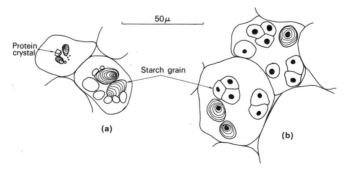

Fig. 3.8 Cells with starch grains. (a) *Solanum tuberosum*, potato. Starch grains are simple with an eccentric hilum. A protein crystal is also present. (b) *Ipomoea batatas*, sweet potato, with some compound grains. Striations are shown in some of the starch grains. × 430.

are characteristic of some plants, e.g. rice, *Oryza sativa*, sweet potato, *Ipomoea batatas* (Fig. 3.8b).

In the starch grains of cereals, the number of striations correspond to the number of days growth, whereas in potato starch the layers are sub-divided into a thick region formed in $18\frac{1}{2}$ hr and a thinner region formed in 2 hr. Experiments in which plants were grown under conditions of constant temperature and continuous light showed that the cereal starches no longer exhibited stratification whereas potato starch still did. Periodicity in the latter is thus apparently independent of external conditions.[119]

Starch grains may be found in all parenchymatous tissues, but especially in storage organs such as tubers, corms, rhizomes, endosperm or cotyledons of seeds. Starch is synthesized by the chloroplasts; it is subsequently broken down and transported as sugar to other parts of the plant, where it is re-synthesized by amyloplasts.

Commercial starches are extracted from various different parts of the plant, e.g. sago starch from stems; potato starch from tubers; wheat, maize and rice starches from seeds; tapioca and cassava starches from roots.

Protein

Proteins sometimes occur as reserve material. Storage proteins may be amorphous or crystalline or may occur in the form of definite bodies, the aleurone grains. Cuboidal crystalloids of protein may be observed in the cells of the peripheral regions of the potato tuber (Fig. 3.8a). Peeling potatoes may thus remove much of the reserve protein, and is nutritionally a bad practice.

Aleurone grains sometimes combine amorphous and crystalloid forms of protein. They are found in many seeds, in the cells of the endosperm and embryo, sometimes occurring in specific layers. An example of this is the aleurone layer of cereals, the outermost layer or layers of the endosperm, just below the coat of the caryopsis.

Aleurone grains are bounded by a proteinaceous membrane which in the simplest type merely encloses a mass of amorphous protein. The more complex types have various inclusions—crystalloids, globoids or crystals of calcium oxalate. For example, the aleurone grains of the castor oil plant, *Ricinus*, usually have one crystalloid and one globoid, those of the nutmeg, *Myristica fragrans*, have only a crystalloid, and those of some members of the Umbelliferae contain a rosette crystal of calcium oxalate.

In general aleurone grains are rather small, smaller than most starch grains. They stain brown with iodine in potassium iodide, and yellow with an alcoholic solution of picric acid.

Plastids concerned with the synthesis of aleurone apparently aggregate in the vacuoles, where their products accumulate to form aleurone grains. Recent work with the electron microscope has confirmed the vacuolar origin of aleurone grains.[45,194] In wheat endosperm, storage proteins are believed to be formed on the ribosomes of the ER and subsequently secreted internally, appearing to be localized in vacuoles.[123] Study with the electron microscope reveals a peripheral bounding membrane—at least in some species—enclosing a ground substance in which, as a rule, little structure is distinguished; in some species, however, electron-dense globoids are observed.[194]

Recently, a function of aleurone-containing cells of great importance to the embryo has been demonstrated. In barley it has been shown that the hormone gibberellic acid (GA) stimulated both germination and the activity of the starch-digesting enzyme amylase. When, after removal of the embryo, slices of endosperm with and without the special aleurone layer characteristic of cereals were treated with GA, it was found that amylase activity was stimulated only in the presence of the aleurone layer.[195] The cells of the aleurone layer specifically respond to GA by secreting α-amylase.[262] Under normal conditions in germinating seeds it is the embryo which produces gibberellin, which stimulates the aleurone layer to produce α-amylase; and this in turn acts upon the starch present in the cells of the endosperm to convert it to sugar, thus rendering it available to the growing embryo. In the language of molecular biology, in this system the gibberellin is acting as an effector which activates the normally repressed genes controlling the synthesis of α-amylase. After treatment with GA, the rates of synthesis of RNA and of protein by the cells of the aleurone layer are approximately doubled, and nearly half of the total protein formed is α-amylase.[33]

Changes in the aleurone grains and their membranes can be observed with the electron microscope as early as 8 hr after treatment with GA, and the changes which occur in fine structure induced by GA in excised aleurone tissue are identical with those occurring during normal germination.[195]

This is a good example of a structurally specialized region which has also a distinctive physiological role in the plant. It is evident that physiological events and structural changes in the tissues are very closely associated.

Fats and oils

Fats and oils are widely distributed in plant cells; they are chemically similar, fats usually being solid and oils liquid, though this is a rather arbitrary distinction. Waxes, cutin and suberin, which occur in and upon the cell wall, are also fatty.

Fats and oils are valuable reserve food materials, and are most commonly found in the tissues of seeds. They occur in the form of solids or as liquid droplets, often dispersed in the cytoplasm of the cell sap. They may be formed by elaioplasts, or by small organelles bounded by a unit membrane, the spherosomes. Fats and oils are frequently located in the cells of the endosperm or perisperm of the seed, but may occur in special layers, e.g. in the second layer below the epidermis in seeds of cardamom (*Elettaria cardamomum*). Essential or volatile oils are usually formed by specialized secretory tissues, and are discussed in Chapter 10.

Oils and fats stain a reddish colour on warming with Sudan III or IV, and are turned black by osmic acid.

Seeds and fruits are important commercial sources of oil. For example, almond, linseed and castor oil are derived respectively from the seeds of *Prunus amygdalus*, *Linum* and *Ricinus*, and olive oil from the fruit of *Olea*.

Crystals

Crystalline deposits in various forms occur in the cells of many plants. Most consist of salts of calcium; the commonest is calcium oxalate, but calcium carbonate also occurs. Crystals are generally considered to constitute depositions of waste products. They are visible as bright objects on a dark background when viewed by polarized light.

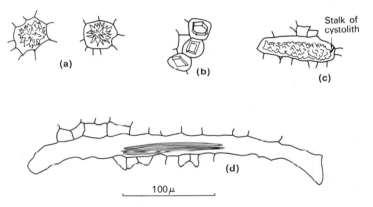

Fig. 3.9 Crystals. (a) Druses from the mesophyll of the leaf of *Salix*. (b) Prismatic crystals from the leaf of *Citrus*. (c) Cystolith from the leaf of *Hygrophila*; the cystolith lies horizontally in the cell (compare Fig. 3.10). (d) Raphides in the petal of *Impatiens*. In (c) and (d) the crystal-containing cells are considerably larger than neighbouring cells. × 245.

There are several different forms of crystals in plants, but all originate from a single crystal. Subsequently crystals may aggregate together.

Single or twin **prisms**, either rectangular prisms or pyramids, may occur (Fig. 3.9b). Prismatic crystals are found in leaves of *Hyoscyamus niger*, *Vicia sativa*, etc., and very large prismatic crystals in the secondary phloem of *Quillaia saponaria*.

Another common form of crystal is the *druse*. These are more or less spherical aggregates of crystals composed of many prisms or pyramids with projecting points all over the surface (Fig. 3.9a). Such crystals are present in the rhizome of rhubarb, *Rheum rhaponticum*, the leaves of *Datura stramonium*, etc.

Rosette crystals are also aggregates having a fairly large, uniform centre. The components are all nearly equal in length, and radiate out from this centre, giving the whole crystal the appearance of a toothed edge. Rosette crystals occur in the aleurone grains of Umbelliferous seeds.

Raphides or acicular crystals are long and needle-shaped, pointed at both ends, and are usually aggregated in bundles. They occur in the cells of the bulbs of squill, *Scilla urginea*, and petals of *Impatiens* (Fig. 3.9d).

Sandy crystals, or crystal sand, are very small crystals frequently massed together. They occur in particular families, e.g. Solanaceae. The individual crystals are often wedge-shaped, or microsphenoidal, in form, as in the leaf of deadly nightshade, *Atropa belladonna*.

The types of crystal described above are usually deposits of calcium oxalate. Specialized depositions of calcium carbonate, known as **cystoliths**, also occur in some species (Figs. 3.9c, 3.10). These consist of depositions of $CaCO_3$ around peg-like ingrowths of the cell wall, and are found in parenchyma and epidermal cells, including trichomes or hairs, e.g. those of the hop, *Humulus lupulus*. In the leaf of *Ficus elastica*, the india rubber plant, cystoliths occur in enlarged epidermal cells known as **lithocysts**. At early stages of leaf development all the epidermal cells appear similar, but slightly later some cells, the future lithocysts, become distinguishable by their denser cytoplasm and larger nucleus. These cells do not divide in harmony with their neighbours, but enlarge while the outer wall thickens and a cellulose stalk develops and projects into the lumen of the cell (Fig. 3.10b, c). Deposition of $CaCO_3$ begins at a relatively late stage of leaf development (Fig. 3.10c, d). The nucleus apparently remains in a functional condition within the lithocyst.[1]

Crystals are most commonly found in the parenchymatous cells of the pith, cortex and secondary phloem. They may be randomly distributed in the cells, or they may occur in **idioblasts**. These are specialized cells which differ from their neighbours in size, contents or function. For example, the bundles of raphides in squill bulb and in the petals of *Impatiens* occur in cells much larger than those around them; the raphide-containing cells may also contain mucilage. The lithocysts of *Ficus* are obviously also idioblasts. There may be one or many crystals in a cell. Crystals may be restricted to or concentrated in the cells of a particular region, e.g. the prismatic crystals in the phloem parenchyma cells surrounding a bundle of fibres in the bark of cascara, *Rhamnus purshianus*, and in the cells adjacent to the veins in leaves of *Vicia sativa*. Such a localized distribution of

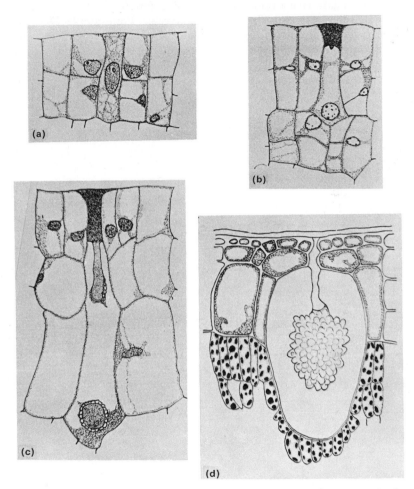

Fig. 3.10 Stages in the development of lithocysts in the leaf of *Ficus elastica*. (a) An incipient lithocyst with enlarged nucleus and dense cytoplasm. (b) The outer wall has thickened and the peg or stalk of the cystolith is just developing. The nucleus is at the bottom of the cell. (c) A late stage in stalk formation. The lithocyst has failed to divide, whereas neighbouring cells have divided. Cytoplasm is aggregated round the nucleus at the base of the cell. (d) Mature lithocyst with deposit of calcium carbonate on the stalk. (a), (b) and (c) ×855. (d) ×700. (From Ajello,[1] Figs. 4, 6, 9 and 17, pp. 590 and 592.)

crystal-containing cells is very interesting, and deserves further investigation. At present the underlying causes are not understood.

Recent studies with the electron microscope have shown that various kinds of crystals have a complex internal structure.[7,8]

Crystals may sometimes be of taxonomic value. For example, Dormer[77] has shown that the crystals in the ovary wall of members of the Compositae vary in form in different species. In a more extensive study of the genus *Centaurea*, he showed[78] that the 112 species studied could be divided into two groups on the basis of crystal form; the crystals were either prismatic or curvilinear.

4

The Cell Wall

The prevailing view of the cell wall is that essentially it is not a living system, but in the absence of the protoplast that formed it is merely a non-living shell. However, it is by no means independent of the cytoplasm.

Formation of the cell wall

The cell wall is formed during the process of cell division. During nuclear division a plate is gradually produced at the position of the equator of the spindle. Work with the electron microscope indicates that vesicles formed by the dictyosomes apparently fuse to form the cell plate[188,275] and the process continues at both ends until the cell plate reaches the existing cell walls. Elements of the endoplasmic reticulum become incorporated into the cell plate at intervals and mark the positions of the future plasmodesmata, the cytoplasmic connections which traverse the wall between adjacent cells.

The precise chemical nature of the cell plate in the early stages of its development is not known, but it gives rise to the middle lamella, which is composed of pectic substances. This layer, which is sometimes called intercellular substance, holds together the primary walls of adjacent cells. It can be dissolved by various substances, including the enzyme pectinase; the various techniques used to macerate plant tissues in order to observe dissociated cells depend upon this fact. Some fungi are able to produce pectinase, and can penetrate plant tissues by causing dissolution of the middle lamella.

Primary cell wall

The primary wall is the first wall to be formed by the cell, and is deposited on either side of the middle lamella by the contiguous cells. Chemically it consists mainly of cellulose, hemicellulose and other polysaccharides. The cellulose lamellae may be separated by layers of pectic substances, for example in the walls of epidermal cells.

All meristematic cells have primary walls, and also many mature cells which still have living contents. Since the wall is formed when the cell is young it must undergo considerable growth; the mechanism by which it grows is discussed below. It is considered that one of the functions of auxin is to increase the plasticity, and thus the extensibility, of the cell wall. The

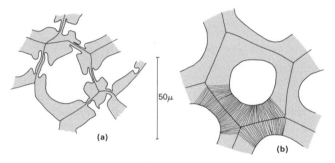

(a)

50μ

(b)

Fig. 4.1 Endosperm cells. (a) *Phoenix dactylifera*, date. (b) *Strychnos nuxvomica*, nux vomica. The thick cellulosic cell walls are stippled. In (a) slightly bordered pits are present in the walls; in (b) some of the numerous plasmodesmata are shown. × 430.

wall may not only undergo surface growth, but may also increase markedly in thickness. Changes of thickness of the primary wall during growth are considered to be reversible, as opposed to the more permanent changes which occur in the secondary wall.[91] The primary walls of some plants, e.g. those of the endosperm in date, *Phoenix dactylifera* (Fig. 4.1), and persimmon, *Diospyros virginiana*, are very thick and serve as a source of reserve carbohydrate.

Secondary cell wall

Where a secondary wall is formed it is deposited on the inner side of the existing wall, next to the cell lumen. It consists of cellulose and other polysaccharides, but hemicelluloses are relatively less important than they are in the primary wall. Hemicelluloses are like cellulose, but are built up, not of glucose molecules, but of those of other sugars. Various other substances, notably lignin, may be deposited in the wall. The structure of lignin is not fully understood; it is not a carbohydrate, but a polymer made up of units of phenylpropane derivatives. Where the secondary wall becomes lignified, the primary wall usually does so also, and indeed lignification commonly begins at the primary wall or the middle lamella. The secondary wall often consists of three layers, so that a cell wall may consist altogether of five layers: the middle lamella, the primary wall and a three-layered secondary wall (Fig. 4.2).

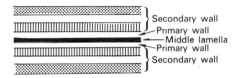

Fig. 4.2   Diagram indicating the structure of two adjacent secondary cell walls.

Secondary walls are usually formed after a cell has completed its elongation, and therefore do not normally extend to any considerable degree. They are generally present in cells which are non-living at maturity, such as sclereids, fibres and vessel elements. In the still elongating elements of the protoxylem the secondary wall is not continuous but is laid down in annular or helical bands; the primary wall between these regions continues to extend and grow harmoniously with the organ in which the elements occur. The reasons for this localized deposition of secondary wall are not fully understood, and require further investigation. The secondary cell wall is considered to provide mechanical strength.

Components and structure of the cell wall

Work with the electron microscope shows that the cellulose in cell walls consists of many fine strands or microfibrils. These may be arranged randomly or in a more or less regular fashion. Within the microfibrils themselves are smaller units, the micelles, which are small aggregations of cellulose molecules that lie parallel to one another and thus confer a crystalline structure upon the microfibrils. More recently it has been claimed that the ultimate structural units of the cell wall are elementary fibrils about 35 Å in diameter, which are not aggregated into larger strands.[189] The spaces between the less regularly arranged molecules in the microfibrils are filled with water, pectic substances, hemicelluloses and, in secondary walls, lignin, cutin, etc.[237] Because of this deposition of lignin between the existing cellulose framework, there is always a swelling of the cell wall during lignification.[187] Recent work has demonstrated the occurrence of a group of proteins containing hydroxyproline in the primary walls of various tissues. The amount present increases during growth, and it is thought that the proteins may serve enzymatic as well as structural functions.[153] Experiments with radioactive isotopes show that protein synthesized in the cytoplasm is regularly transported into the cell wall. The protein may be involved in orientation of the fibrils.[189] Other workers consider that the wall protein plays an important role in cell extension.[161]

The fatty substance cutin is found in association with most epidermal cell walls. The cuticular membrane is composed of a cutinized layer, a layer of cellulose encrusted with cutin, and an outer cuticularized layer or cuticle consisting of cutin adcrusted on the cell wall (Fig. 4.3).[237] The

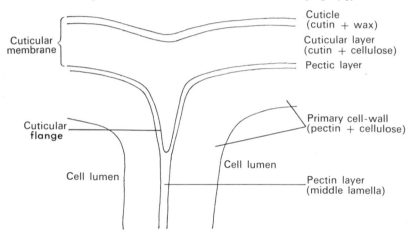

Fig. 4.3 Diagram illustrating the structure of two cuticularized epidermal cell walls at their junction. (From Stace,[237] Fig. 13, p. 63.)

boundary between the cellulose layer and the cutin is sharply delineated by a layer of pectin (Fig. 4.4).[187] The cuticular layer may produce cuticular pegs between the walls of adjacent epidermal cells. No internal structure has been observed in the cutin itself. Wax may be present on the surface of the epidermis in leaves and fruits (see Chapter 7).

In some cells, notably those of the phellem or cork (see Chapter 11), the walls are encrusted with another fatty substance, suberin. This contains no cellulose.

The microfibrils are oriented in various ways in cell walls, usually more regularly in the secondary wall. In the primary wall the microfibrils are often oriented in a direction more or less transverse to the long axis; they become arranged more longitudinally during growth of the cell. As subsequent wall layers are formed the microfibrils come to be oriented more and

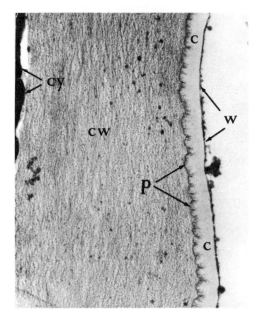

Fig. 4.4 Section through the cell wall of leaf epidermis of *Plantago major*·
c, cutin; cw, cell wall; cy, cytoplasm of cell; p, dark layer of pectic material; w,
dark layer of wax.   × 22,000.·(By courtesy of Dr. D. A. Fisher.)

more longitudinally. This transition is gradual; the change in direction of
the microfibrils in successive wall layers may be about 120° (Fig. 4.5). As
the last stage of wall formation, a tertiary wall may be formed; this differs
from the primary and secondary ones and is probably not cellulosic. In
gymnosperms this layer may be covered with warts. In the cotton hair, the
subject of much work on the cell wall, there is a gradual transition from an
approximately axial orientation of microfibrils on the outer surface,
through a central region of crossed microfibrils to the transverse orientation
of the inner layer (Fig. 4.6).[207]

In the cells of different regions of a developing organ the walls may show
differential orientations of the microfibrils. For example, in the root of
onion (*Allium cepa*) the cell walls of the apical initials show a loosely woven
mesh of microfibrils; in slightly older cells the microfibrils are mainly
aligned horizontally, and this holds true also during active elongation. But
in older elongating cells the pattern changes, and an interwoven mesh of
microfibrils is again present. In the root hair zone of the root successive
sheets of helical microfibrils, alternately clockwise and anticlockwise,
resulting in a criss-cross pattern, are deposited.[221]

3

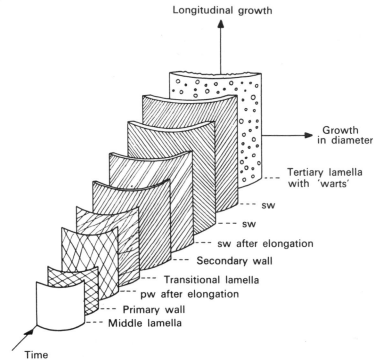

Longitudinal growth

Growth
in diameter

Tertiary lamella
with 'warts'

--- sw

--- sw

--- sw after elongation

--- Secondary wall

--- Transitional lamella

--- pw after elongation

--- Primary wall
--- Middle lamella

Time

Fig. 4.5 Time sequence of the cell wall layers in a tracheid. pw, primary wall; sw, secondary wall. (From Mühlethaler,[187] Fig. 8, p. 105.)

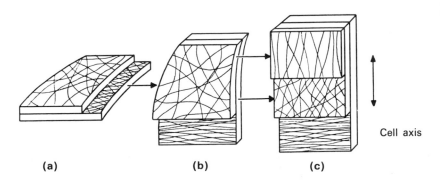

Cell axis

(a)   (b)   (c)

Fig. 4.6 Multi-net growth of the cell wall in a growing cotton hair. (a) Near the tip; (b) where the tip merges into the tubular part of the hair; (c) in the tubular part. The transition is more gradual than the diagram indicates. (From Mühlethaler,[187] Fig. 13, p. 112; after Houwink and Roelofsen (1954).)

Another interesting study on the onion root[146] reveals that these changes in wall structure can apparently be correlated with changes in the relative amounts of cell wall components both in cells at different stages of development, i.e. at different distances from the root tip, and in cells of the different tissues at any one level (Fig. 4.7). In particular, the transitional region between radial enlargement and rapid elongation of the root is characterized by changing relationships between wall components.

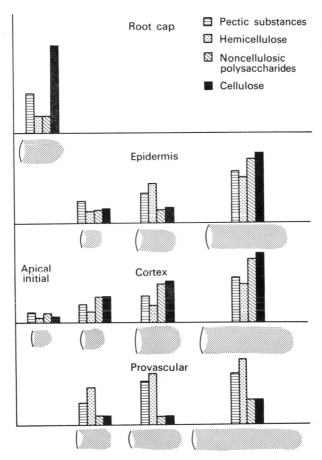

Fig. 4.7 Constituents of the cell wall in the various tissues of a developing root of onion, *Allium cepa*, based on quantitative histochemical procedures and cyto-chemical data. Outlines of stages of cell development in the various tissues are given on the horizontal axis. (From Jensen,[146] Fig. 4–6, p. 101.)

Northcote[192] has pointed out that the synthesis of material and the extent of enlargement of the cell wall during development can be influenced by the nutrition of the growing cell. Factors affecting growth are thus important in affecting the structure and growth of the cell wall.

Growth of the cell wall

Formerly two theories were held regarding how the cell wall grows in thickness: that of growth by *intussusception*, where new microfibrils were held to be laid down between existing microfibrils (Fig. 4.8a), and

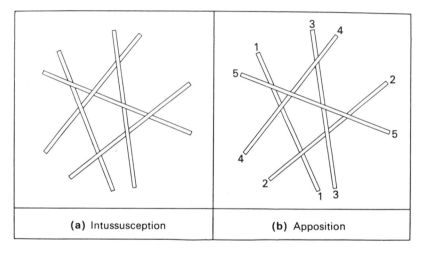

(a) Intussusception   (b) Apposition

Fig. 4.8   Microfibrils in a primary cell wall. Diagrams showing growth by (a) intussusception and (b) apposition. The first formed fibril is 1, the second 2, etc. (From Mühlethaler,[187] Fig. 7, p. 103.)

that of growth by *apposition*, where new microfibrils were laid down on top of existing ones, forming a new layer (Fig. 4.8b). It is now considered that the formation of both primary and secondary cell walls occurs principally by the mechanism of apposition.[187] It is probable, however, that some growth by intussusception does occur. Growth by apposition is shown convincingly in the successive lamellae visible in some secondary walls, e.g. those of cotton hairs and phloem fibres (Fig. 4.6).[207] Deposition of cellulose uniformly over the whole surface of the cell has been demonstrated by the use of the radioactive isotope ^{14}C; this was incorporated into the whole length of the primary cell wall.[207]

With respect to longitudinal growth, the theory now most widely held is the ***multi-net*** theory of cell wall growth; this accounts also for the observed orientation of the microfibrils in successive layers of the wall. On this view microfibrils are first deposited more or less transversely to the long axis of the cell, and this layer is later pushed outwards as a result of the formation by apposition of a layer internal to it. During cell elongation the first-formed layers of microfibrils are stretched and thus become oriented in a progressively more longitudinal plane (Fig. 4.6). Recent studies of cell wall formation in fibres and tracheids using the electron microscope (Fig. 4.5), and also the technique of autoradiography whereby the path of radioactive isotopes is followed, are consistent with the multi-net theory of cell wall growth.[207] As in earlier work with primary cell walls, labelled carbon was found to be deposited more or less uniformly over the secondary walls of fibres and tracheids.

In fibres the formation of the secondary wall may begin near the centre of the cell and progress towards the tips. The wall is thus thicker near the centre.

In some cells, e.g. root hairs, pollen tubes, tracheids and fibres, growth occurs only at the tip.[207] This tip growth is regarded as a localized type of multi-net growth. The role of determining whether the wall of the whole cell will grow or only a localized part of it—as, for example, in root hairs or stellate parenchyma cells—is attributed to the cytoplasm.[208]

Intercellular spaces

In mature tissues, spaces are frequently present between cells. These spaces are formed by a splitting apart of the walls of contiguous cells, and are therefore said to be schizogenous. In many plants growing in aquatic habitats a complex continuous system of well developed intercellular air spaces is present. Even in terrestrial plants, intercellular spaces sometimes become enlarged and give rise to secretory glands or ducts (see Chapter 10).

In meristematic regions the cells are usually thought to be in close contact all round. Observation of the onion root tip with the electron microscope, however, revealed the presence of intercellular spaces only 20 μ from the root apex.[221] Thus very small spaces may exist between cells even where they are not readily observed with the light microscope.

Plasmodesmata

Thin strands of cytoplasm, the plasmodesmata, pass through the cell walls at intervals, thus connecting the living protoplasts of adjacent cells. The plasmodesmata sometimes occur in the future sites of primary pit fields (see below), but may be randomly distributed through the wall. They can often be observed traversing the thick cell walls of the endosperm of certain seeds (Fig. 4.1), e.g. date, *Phoenix dactylifera*, coffee, *Coffea arabica*. Plasmodesmata are evident in cell walls viewed with the electron microscope; they may be very numerous. The endoplasmic reticulum has been seen to connect with the plasmodesmata, thus forming a membrane system that can link nuclei of adjacent cells.

A recent staining technique which has been devised to show the existence of plasmodesmata in the walls of living cells—formerly impossible to demonstrate—indicates that they do have a real existence and are not artifacts attributable to treatment.[167]

Pits

The primary cell walls are usually not of uniform thickness but have conspicuous depressions in them at intervals; these are called primary pit fields. Secondary walls also have cavities of various kinds, the pits. However thin the wall may be in the area of the pits or primary pit fields, it always forms a continuous membrane across these regions; actual holes or pores in the wall large enough to be visible with the light microscope are uncommon. Plasmodesmata traverse the primary pit fields, but may occur in other regions of the wall also. The pits may correspond in position to the primary pit fields of an earlier stage in wall development, but this topographic correspondence is by no means absolute. No thickening is laid down over the primary wall in the region of the pit, i.e. the secondary wall is completely interrupted.

A pit consists of a pit cavity and a pit-closing membrane, which comprises the middle lamella and a thin layer of primary wall. Where pits in the walls of adjacent cells correspond in position, as they frequently do, a

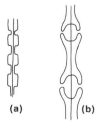

(a)   (b)

Fig. 4.9 Structure of simple and bordered pits as seen in longitudinal section. (a) Simple; (b) bordered.

pit-pair is formed, and the pit-closing membrane consists of the middle lamella and the primary walls of both cells. Pits may be divided into two main types: simple pits, in which the secondary wall does not arch over the pit cavity, and bordered pits, in which it does (Fig. 4.9).

Simple pits

Conspicuous areas of simple pits may be present in the walls of certain parenchymatous cells, e.g. those of the pulp of the fruit of *Citrullus colocynthis*, or the pith of the stem of elder, *Sambucus nigra*. In some simple pits, especially those found in thick-walled sclereids, the pit cavities may branch, although the opening to the interior of the cell, the pit aperture, is always simple. Such pits are called ramiform pits (Fig. 6.1).

The pit cavity may be of uniform width throughout, or it may be wider or narrower where it abuts upon the lumen of the cell. If it becomes narrower at the end towards the lumen, it is approaching the structure typical of a bordered pit.

In the cells of the onion root tip as many as six or seven primary pit fields per square micron may be present in the walls. This means that a meristematic cell 20 μ long on each side could possess of the order of 20,000 cytoplasmic connections with adjacent cells, passing through the primary pit fields. During cell growth the number of primary pit fields may remain constant, the distance between them increasing.[187] This is another indication that in most cells growth occurs over the whole of the primary wall.

These primary pit fields in the cells of the onion root tip can be observed first as minute circular depressions in the walls of the apical initials. Under the electron microscope it can be seen that in the young stages each primary pit field consists of numerous pores, some of which contain the remains of plasmodesmata, which, however, are not restricted to the primary pit fields. In the region of elongation the pits may be divided into two or more sections by strands of microfibrils. In the final stage of development of the pit it is subdivided in this way into two sections, each with several clearly defined pores between the microfibrils.[221] These pores are, of course, extremely small, and are not visible with the light microscope.

Bordered pits

These usually occur in the elements of the xylem, e.g. vessels, tracheids, fibres, and are more complex in structure than simple pits. The secondary wall arches over the pit cavity, forming the pit border. This encloses the pit chamber, which opens into the cell lumen through the pit aperture (Figs. 4.9, 4.10). The torus is a thickened area on the pit membrane which is present in gymnosperms. If the wall is very thick there may also be a pit canal leading from the cell lumen into the pit chamber. There is then an outer aperture, towards the cell wall, and an inner aperture towards the cell lumen. The latter is variable in shape; the thicker the cell wall the longer and narrower is the inner aperture, and it may even be slit-like in shape. When this occurs the two apertures often cross one another, giving the 'cross pits' frequently seen in lignified fibres or tracheids.

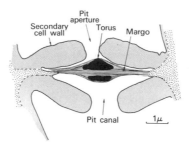

Fig. 4.10   Cross section through a bordered pit of a transfusion tracheid from a needle of *Pinus sylvestris*, showing the pit membrane. The torus (black) is covered on both sides by microfibrils originating from the margo. The secondary wall is lightly stippled, the lignified rim of the pit chamber dotted. (Drawn from an electron micrograph of Liese,[165] Fig. 17, p. 287.)

Bordered pits in tracheids can act as valves which control the flow of water through the cell; they thus assume some physiological importance in the plant. The torus acts as a stopper in the valve. If the fluids move too rapidly through the pit, the torus is pushed into a position where it rests against the pit border, preventing further flow.[187] The structure of the pit membrane is important in understanding the mechanism for entry of fluids. The torus, which is apparently impermeable, is suspended by loosely arranged, radially oriented groups of microfibrils which form the raised border of the pit membrane, known as the margo; small perforations occur in this region (Figs. 4.10, 4.11). This structure of the pit membrane, which has recently been confirmed in studies with the electron microscope,[165,259] was postulated in its entirety by Bailey in 1913, on the basis of light microscope observations and experiments on the passage of an aqueous suspension of carbon particles through the woody tissues.[21] This is one good illustration of the fact that the skill, ingenuity and insight of the research worker are more important than the possession of elaborate equipment. Much valuable work can be done with very simple tools, such as are readily available in any school or college laboratory. Access to more elaborate equipment, however, may make the research work easier and permit a more certain interpretation of the results.

In the bordered pits of angiospermous woods (hardwoods) both the pit canal and the pit chamber are lined by tertiary wall. Plasmodesmata are usually present in pit membranes which separate living cells. In some dicotyledons, vestured pits occur; these are characterized by small outgrowths from the pit wall which project into the pit cavity.[268] These vestures apparently consist of accumulations of cytoplasmic material at the cell wall, which are covered by the warty layer.[215]

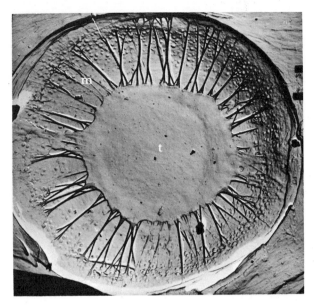

Fig. 4.11 Bordered pit of *Pinus sylvestris*, showing the torus (t) and margo (m) with radiating fibrils.   × 5,000. (From Mühlethaler,[187] Fig. 31, p. 122.)

The arrangement of pits in a cell or element may vary considerably. There are three main types of arrangement: scalariform (ladder-like), opposite and alternate. Recent work suggests, however, that one arrangement may readily change to another during growth and development.[26]

5

Parenchyma and Collenchyma

PARENCHYMA

Much of the discussion of the plant cell in the preceding chapters is relevant to parenchyma, the most basic type of differentiated cell. Parenchyma cells are usually relatively unspecialized. They form the ground tissue of plants, and occur in the pith and cortex of stems and roots, the mesophyll of the leaf, the endosperm of the seed, the flesh of fruits and in the medullary rays. Parenchymatous cells are also present in association with the conducting elements of the primary and secondary xylem and phloem. Their origin may thus be diverse: from the apical meristems of stem or root, the marginal meristems of leaves, or from the vascular cambium or even the phellogen in more mature organs with secondary growth.

Parenchyma consists usually of thin-walled, vacuolated cells with living protoplasts; the cells are often, but by no means always, more or less isodiametric. The topographic situation of these cells within the plant, outlined above, gives some indication of the importance of parenchymatous cells in many functional activities. Examples of these are photosynthesis, respiration, secretion, and storage of food materials of various types. The contents of parenchyma cells may include crystals, tannins, oils and other secretions, starch, aleurone grains and plastids. Parenchyma which contains numerous chloroplasts and is concerned principally with photosynthesis may be termed *chlorenchyma*. It may be found not only in leaves but frequently also in the peripheral regions of young stems. Food material may be stored not only in cell inclusions such as aleurone grains or starch grains within the cell (Fig. 3.8), but also sometimes in the thick cell walls of the endosperm of certain seeds, e.g. *Strychnos nux-vomica, Diospyros virginiana* (persimmon) or *Phoenix dactylifera*, the date (Fig. 4.1). The hemicelluloses within the thick walls of these cells may be regarded as reserve materials. The walls of such endosperm cells, although thick, are primary walls, but parenchyma cells may sometimes have secondary, lignified walls, as in secondary xylem and, occasionally, pith parenchyma.

Although parenchyma cells are usually described as isodiametric, their shape is by no means simple. In isolation, parenchyma cells may be more or less spherical, but when they form part of a tissue various forces act upon them and affect their form. They are in fact polyhedral, having many facets along which they are in contact with neighbouring cells; ideally, they have 14 sides or facets (Fig. 5.1).[139] It is thought that both pressure

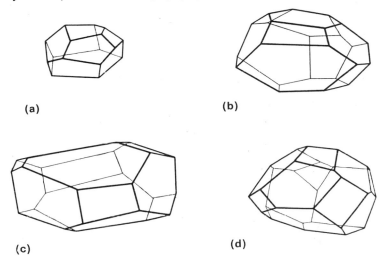

(a)

(b)

(c)

(d)

Fig. 5.1 Cells of the pith of *Ailanthus*. (a) Small cell with 10 faces. (b) and (c) Cells with 14 faces. (d) Cell with 17 faces. × 200. (From Hulbary,[139] Figs. 1, 5, 7 and 10, p. 564.)

and the forces of surface tension play a part in influencing the shape of a cell within a tissue. Parenchyma cells may be considerably elongated in one plane, as in the cells of the palisade tissue in the leaf, or they may have several 'arms' or branches, as in the 'stellate' parenchyma cells of the mesophyll of leaves of *Canna* or the pith of *Juncus* (Fig. 5.2). The effect of mechanical stretching during growth on the intercellular spaces between these cells apparently leads to the first stage in the development of the arms of the cells.[121] The arms evidently undergo elongation throughout their entire length, not just in regions close to the spaces.

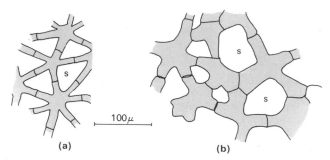

(a)   (b)

Fig. 5.2 'Armed' or branched parenchyma cells. (a) From the pith of *Juncus*. (b) From the midrib of the leaf of *Canna*. Large intercellular spaces (s) are present. × 155.

Intercellular spaces arise either by the splitting apart of the middle lamella region between cells, or, less frequently, by breakdown or lysis of the cells. In certain tissues, notably those of many aquatic plants, intercellular spaces may be exceptionally well developed and form a connected system throughout the entire plant. This tissue is often called aerenchyma, a term reserved by other workers for a tissue in aquatic plants derived from a phellogen. It was formerly believed that this tissue with abundant air spaces functioned in aeration and in giving buoyancy to aquatic plants; more recently, it has been pointed out that such a system is characterized by exceptional strength for a minimum amount of tissue, and it has been suggested that the honeycomb-like system of intercellular spaces could be an efficient way of withstanding the considerable mechanical stress to which plants in an aquatic environment may well be subjected.[283] However, at least for plants rooted in waterlogged soils, the air space system probably is important in aeration.[59]

Although relatively unspecialized in the normal development, seeming one of the less interesting tissues, because of their living protoplasts parenchyma cells retain the potentiality for the resumption of meristematic activity, and thus possess striking versatility. Thus, if in horticultural practice an organ is excised from the plant and used as a cutting, it is usually from the parenchyma cells present in that organ that the new root or bud primordia develop. Perhaps the best example of the potentialities of parenchyma cells when removed from their normal environment is the development of whole carrot plants from phloem parenchyma cells of the carrot root, described in Chapter 2. A parenchyma cell, or a small group of such cells, thus possesses the capacity to develop into a whole plant with a complete set of differentiated tissues, but is normally prevented from developing in this way by the restrictions imposed by its position within the plant.

COLLENCHYMA

Collenchyma cells have living protoplasts and thickened cellulosic walls. They are extensible cells with a considerable degree of plasticity, and function as supporting tissue in growing organs. They may contain chloroplasts and carry out photosynthesis. They thus differ from parenchymatous cells chiefly in their thick-walled nature, and in being usually somewhat elongated in a plane parallel to the long axis of the organ in which they occur.

Individual collenchyma cells may attain lengths of 2 mm, though rarely. Collenchyma cells differ from sclerenchymatous fibres both in their possession of living contents at maturity and in the cellulosic nature of their walls. Thus collenchyma will not stain red with phloroglucinol and hydrochloric acid, a test for lignin, but will stain blue if treated with a solution of iodine in potassium iodide followed by 66% sulphuric acid, a test for cellulose. In later stages of development, however, collenchyma cells may occasionally become lignified. Collenchyma usually occupies a peripheral position in the organs in which it occurs. In stems it may lie immediately beneath the epidermis, or below a few outer layers of parenchyma. The collenchymatous cells may form a complete cylinder near the periphery of the stem or they may occur in the form of discrete strands, especially in ridged structures such as the petiole of celery, *Apium graveolens*, or many stems (*Calendula, Senecio*). Collenchymatous strengthening tissue is commonly found in stems, petioles, peduncles and pedicels; it occurs only rarely in roots, but more frequently in those which have been exposed to the light.[80]

It is often difficult to be certain whether the collenchyma originates from the procambium or from the meristem giving rise to the ground tissue. In the petiole of celery, for example, active periclinal divisions occur on the abaxial side of the procambial strands. These cells become arranged in radial rows and divide, forming a column of elongated, densely staining cells which is separated from the true procambial strand by a secretory duct. This outer column of cells differentiates to form collenchyma.[84] During development, the elongated collenchyma cells may divide transversely, thus having a superficial resemblance to septate fibres.

Usually wall thickening begins in the corners of the cells, but it may spread from there in various ways in different species. In addition to collenchyma cells with more or less uniformly thickened walls, three main types of collenchyma are recognized, according to the disposition of the wall thickening. These are: (i) *angular* collenchyma, the commonest type, in which the wall thickening is deposited predominantly at the corners, or angles of the cells, e.g. celery petiole, stems of *Dahlia, Datura*; (ii) *lamellar* collenchyma, in which the thickening is deposited more heavily on the tangential than on the radial walls of the cells, e.g. stems of *Sambucus*, *Rhamnus*; and (iii) *lacunar* collenchyma, in which the thickening is deposited primarily around the intercellular spaces between the cells, e.g. petioles of *Petasites*, aerial roots of *Monstera*. Examples of these various types are illustrated in Fig. 5.3. The mechanism controlling this differential deposition of wall thickening is apparently not understood; it must be a particularly interesting one, because of these various extremely characteristic patterns of thickening.

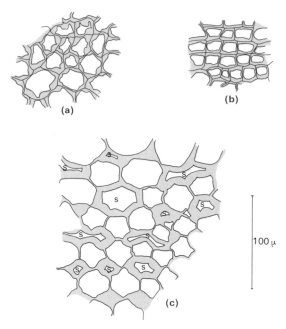

Fig. 5.3 Types of collenchyma. (a) Angular collenchyma from the stem of *Cucurbita*. (b) Lamellar collenchyma from the stem of *Sambucus*. (c) Lacunar collenchyma from the petiole of *Petasites*. s, intercellular space. × 240.

In collenchymatous cell walls there are high amounts of pectin and hemicelluloses. For example, the collenchyma of *Petasites* was found to consist of 45% pectin and 35% hemicellulose, leaving a maximum of 20% cellulose.[207] The micelles of the cell wall are apparently fairly regularly oriented in an axial plane. In celery, studies with the electron microscope show that the wall thickenings are composed of alternate layers of longitudinally oriented cellulose microfibrils and of non-cellulosic material.[23]

Although there is still abundant scope for a study of the factors control-

(a)   (c)   (e)   (g)

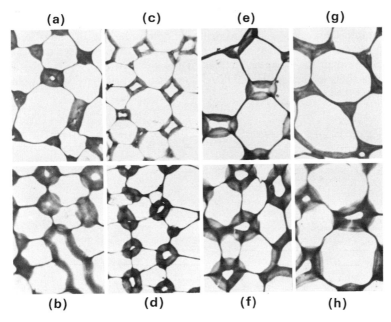

(b)   (d)   (f)   (h)

Fig. 5.4 Sections of the stem and petiole of control and agitated plants of *Datura stramonium*. Above, control; below, agitated. (a), (b) Petiole; (c), (d) 4th internode; (e), (f) 3rd internode; (g), (h) 2nd internode. × 160. (From Walker,[266] Figs. 6–13, p. 720.)

ling the development of collenchyma, a few exploratory experiments have been carried out, and are described below. For example, experiments have shown that mechanical shaking of the plant has a considerable effect on the amount of wall thickening in collenchyma; it does not affect the type of collenchyma formed. In the petioles of celery plants maintained on a mechanical agitator for 9 hours a day over a period of 27 days, 100% more tissue differentiated as collenchyma than in the petioles of control plants. The walls were also 42% thicker.[265] Increases of more than 100% in wall thickness were also obtained in the collenchyma of plants of *Datura stramonium* subjected to comparable treatment for 40 days (Fig. 5.4).[266] It is considered that this stimulation of wall thickening is probably accompanied by inhibition of the elongation of collenchyma cells. The development of collenchyma may thus be affected by certain experimental treatments, but the factors controlling its initial differentiation remain to be elucidated. It would be interesting to subject both species that normally do have collenchyma, and some that normally do not, to mechanical agitation during the whole of their ontogeny from the time of germination.

Collenchyma constitutes a living, flexible tissue which possesses considerable tensile stress. Experiments to determine the breaking load of the strands showed that the collenchyma strands in celery were much stronger than the vascular bundles of the same petiole.[84] The plasticity of the walls of fresh collenchyma cells is also higher than that of phloem fibres.[207]

6

Sclerenchyma

This tissue consists of thick-walled elements, which are normally hard and lignified. The cell walls are thickened secondary walls and the cells usually have no living protoplasts when mature. Sclerenchyma is distinguishable from collenchyma both in this lack of living contents and in being lignified; it has a similar function in the plant, however, namely that of support.

Sclerenchyma may be sub-divided into sclereids and fibres; in general, fibres are much more elongated than sclereids, but many intermediate forms occur.

SCLEREIDS

Sclereids, which are sometimes called stone cells because of their hard walls, are usually much more isodiametric in shape than fibres. The gritty texture of the fruit of *Pyrus*, the pear, is attributable to groups of isodiametric sclereids in the flesh. Usually one diameter is not more than three times the size of the other, but some sclereids, called trichosclereids from their superficial resemblance to trichomes, or hairs, are very long (up to ten times as long as broad) and thus do not fit this description. Such sclereids occur in the leaves of *Olea*, the olive. Sclereids are, indeed, extremely variable in shape, and both on this account and because of their distribution within the plant are exceedingly interesting cells. They occur singly or in groups, sometimes associated with the xylem or phloem (e.g. in bark of *Cinnamomum*, cinnamon) but more commonly in parenchymatous tissues, for example the pith and cortex of stems and petioles, e.g. *Hoya*, or of roots, e.g. *Nymphaea* (water lily), the leaf mesophyll, e.g. *Trochodendron*, *Nymphaea*, the flesh of fruits, e.g. *Pyrus* (pear), the seed coat, e.g. *Pisum* (pea), *Phaseolus* (bean). They may occupy a complete layer, as in the seed coat, but more commonly they occur as idioblasts in the tissues mentioned. The question of what causes the differentiation of these often scattered, isolated cells into sclereids is of great interest, and is open to experimental investigation. The distribution of the sclereids may be apparently random, as in the leaves of *Pseudotsuga* and *Trochodendron*[248] and pear fruits,[249] or they may occur in specific positions, for example at the ends of the veinlets, as in leaves of *Mouriria*,[115] *Boronia*[117] and many of the Magnoliaceae.[260] These last are known as terminal sclereids. In the leaves of *Camellia* sclereids occur predominantly near the margins of the leaf.[111]

Types of sclereid

Sclereids may be classified into a number of types, usually based on the extraordinary variation in form found in these cells.

Brachysclereids are shaped like parenchyma cells and are sometimes called stone cells. They occur in the flesh of fruits, e.g. *Pyrus* (pear),

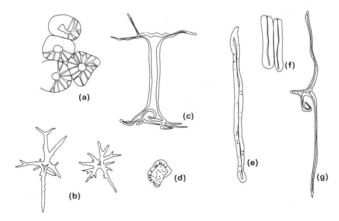

Fig. 6.1   Types of sclereid. (**a**) Brachysclereids from the flesh of pear, *Pyrus*. Note ramiform pits.   × 180. (**b**) Astrosclereids from the leaf of *Trochodendron*. × 50. (After Foster, A. S. (1945), *J. Arnold Arbor.*, **26**, 155–162, Pl. III, Figs. 10 and 13). (**c**) Osteosclereid from the leaf of *Hakea*.   × 115. (**d**) Brachysclereid with uneven wall thickening from the cortex of *Cinnamomum* stem. × 115. (**e**) Macrosclereid from the endocarp of apple, *Malus*.   × 115. (**f**) Macrosclereids from the testa of pea, *Pisum*.   × 180. (**g**) Trichosclereid from the leaf of *Olea*. × 50. (After Arzee,[13] Fig. 8D, p. 685.)

Chaenomeles (quince), and in parenchymatous tissues or phloem of stems, e.g. *Cinnamomum, Hoya.*

Macrosclereids are elongated and columnar in shape, and occur in the seed coat of peas and beans.

Osteosclereids are again columnar but somewhat enlarged at the ends, like a marrow bone, as the name suggests. These again occur in seed coats and in leaves, e.g. *Hakea.*

Astrosclereids are branched and more or less star-shaped. They occur in petioles and leaves, e.g. *Thea* (tea), *Trochodendron, Nymphaea.*

Trichosclereids are very much elongated sclereids, somewhat hair-like in form, and sometimes branched. They occur in aerial roots of *Monstera* and in the leaves of *Olea*, olive.

Examples of these types of sclereid are illustrated in Fig. 6.1.

Origin and development

Sclereids which are randomly distributed are usually formed from parenchyma cells which first become distinguishable from adjacent cells by the large size of their nuclei.[13,120,248] Subsequently these cells grow very rapidly and may send out branches into neighbouring intercellular spaces. Any part of the wall surface may participate in this growth. In the petiole of *Nymphaea*, the water lily, branches of the sclereid grow in the intercellular spaces, and T-shaped sclereids may develop; if the sclereid initial branches into two intercellular spaces, H-shaped sclereids may result (Fig. 6.2d–g).[120] In the root of *N. mexicana*, occasional cortical cells develop as sclereids. These are essentially cubical cells which develop eight branches or prongs at the corners of the cube (Fig. 6.3). Again, these branches grow out into the spaces between the rows of cortical cells. (Being aquatic plants, water lilies have a well developed system of intercellular spaces). The final form of sclereids may thus depend in part on the disposition and ease of penetration of neighbouring tissues. The secondary wall is laid down as the sclereid matures, and may eventually be very thick. Terminal sclereids, associated with the veinlet endings in the leaf mesophyll, are apparently formed from the same cell layer in the meristem that gives rise to the associated procambial strand forming the veinlet.[115] The formation of the sclereid initials thus coincides with the order of differentiation and maturation of the ultimate veinlets.[117]

In the aerial roots of *Monstera*, the initials of the trichosclereids are formed by unequal, polarized divisions at the proximal end of files of cortical cells.[30] The small cells thus formed have dense contents and large nuclei and branches from them grow rapidly into the intercellular system (Fig. 6.2a–c). This is another example of the important consequences in differentiation of unequal, polarized cell divisions (see Chapter 2).

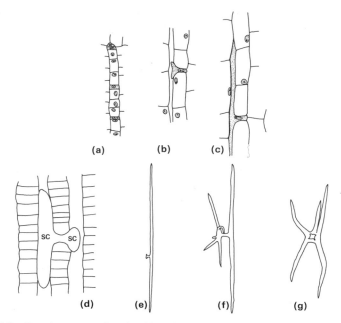

Fig. 6.2 Development of sclereids. (a)–(c) Longitudinal section of root meristem of *Monstera*. (a) Formation of trichosclereids (dotted) at basal ends of cell files. (b) 2200 μ from the root apex, showing the outgrowth of processes into an intercellular space. (c) Later stage. × 120. (After Bloch,[30] Figs. 5–7, p. 546.) (d)–(g) *Nymphaea odorata*. (d) Longitudinal section of petiole of a young leaf showing elongation of a young sclereid (sc) in the intercellular spaces. × 215. (e) Bipolar, (f) double bipolar, and (g) stellate sclereids from mature petioles. × 67. (Drawn from photographs of Gaudet,[120] Figs. 5–7 and 15, p. 527.)

Sclereids are thick-walled, but the thickness of the wall may not be uniform. In the brick-shaped stone cells in cinnamon bark, for example, the inner tangential walls are the most strongly thickened (Fig. 6.1d). The walls of sclereids may have numerous pits, which are usually simple; these are often ramiform, i.e. the pit canal is branched. Most sclereids are lignified, and will stain red with phloroglucinol and hydrochloric acid.

Factors controlling differentiation

The facts that sclereids may originate in so many different ways, and may occur in so many different tissues, emphasize the problem of discovering the factors that influence their formation and development. The whole question of what controls the differentiation of idioblasts (e.g. crystal-containing cells, tracheioidal cells, sclereids, secretory cells,

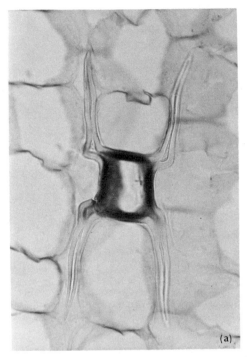
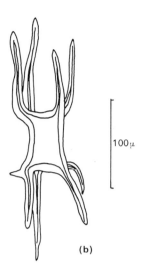

(a)   (b)

Fig. 6.3 Sclereids from the cortex of the root of *Nymphaea mexicana*. (a) Sclereid in longitudinal section of root, showing the position of the outgrowths in the intercellular spaces of the cortical tissue.   × 300. (b) Drawing of an isolated sclereid, showing the 8 outgrowths from the corners of the cell.   × 230.

hairs) is an important one and has been as yet relatively little investigated.

In some tissues, sclereids apparently differentiate when in close proximity to a surface. This is true of brachysclereids in the aerial roots of *Monstera*,[228] and of astrosclereids in the leaf of *Camellia*, where additional sclereids could be induced to form along new surfaces resulting from experimental incisions in the leaves.[111] Differentiation of sclereids from parenchyma cells was induced by wounding in both leaves and aerial roots of *Monstera*.[29] In excised buds of *Trochodendron* grown in sterile culture, sclereids were found to differentiate first along the margins of developing leaves (Fig. 6.4). The influence of the position of a cell within the plant on its future differentiation, discussed in Chapter 2, is again illustrated by these examples.

Some other observations and experiments seem to implicate other

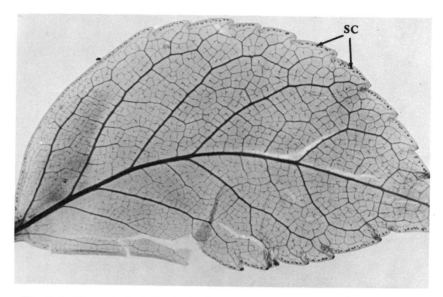

Fig. 6.4 Young leaf of *Trochodendron aralioides*, cleared and stained, from a shoot tip grown in sterile culture. Astrosclereids (sc) are present in the mesophyll at the margin of the leaf only. × 8.

factors. For example, it was found that fewer sclereids developed in detached, cultured leaves of *Camellia* when they were grown in a medium with high concentrations of sucrose, or in medium with the control level of sucrose plus added mannitol,[110] suggesting that osmotic pressure might be a factor affecting sclereid differentiation. In pear fruits, differentiating sclereids appear to stimulate adjacent cells to develop in like manner.[249] A recent observation that in *Rauwolfia* differentiating sclereid initials at various stages of development showed intensified activity of the enzyme cytochrome oxidase[181] is interesting, but may indicate merely that the cells which later differentiate as sclereids have a higher degree of metabolic activity than their neighbours.

Some interesting observations and experiments on leaves of Douglas fir, *Pseudotsuga*, suggest that hormonal factors in the developing plant may affect sclereid formation, and play a role in determining when and where sclereid initials will develop.[5] Observation of the leaves along the branches showed that there were more sclereids per leaf in the basal regions of each year's growth than in the terminal regions (Fig. 6.5). This pattern was repeated each year, for example in a 4-year-old branch (Fig. 6.6). These observations suggest that expanding leaves may affect sclereid formation in the younger developing leaves of a branch. It was shown that complete

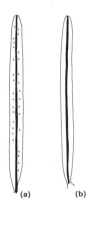

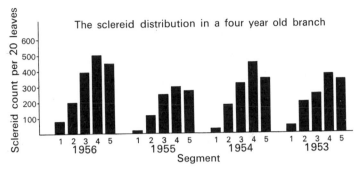

Fig. 6.5 Diagrams of cleared leaves of *Pseudotsuga menziesii*. (a) From the basal part of a 1-year-old branch. Abundant stellate-shaped sclereids (indicated by x) were present. (b) From the uppermost part of a 1-year-old branch. No sclereids were present. ×1. (Drawn from photographs of Al-Talib and Torrey,[5] Figs. 2 and 3, p. 72.)

(a)   (b)

Fig. 6.6 Pattern of sclereid distribution along the axis of a 4-year-old branch of *Pseudotsuga menziesii*. Each segment (1–5) contained approximately 20 leaves. (From Al-Talib and Torrey,[5] Fig. 4, p. 74.)

defoliation of a branch, or removal of the leaves from its upper half, caused premature expansion of next year's leaves from the terminal bud. These leaves did not contain sclereids at the time of removal of the outer leaves, but formed them on expansion. They thus provided good experimental material, since the degree of sclereid formation after various treatments could be studied in them. For example, if lanolin paste containing the auxin indoleacetic acid was applied to the defoliated branches, sclereid formation was considerably inhibited in the developing leaves. In other experiments it was shown that in buds of *Pseudotsuga* grown in culture relatively few sclereids developed in the leaves; but in the presence of higher concentrations of various auxins in the culture medium even this number was reduced.[4] It thus appears that auxin may inhibit sclereid formation at certain concentrations, and it seems possible that the auxin produced by expanding leaves may affect differentiation in younger leaves of the bud.

If it is true that hormonal or osmotic factors in the developing leaf play a part in determining how, when and where sclereid initials will develop, then observations on the distribution and development of mature sclereids in the leaves of such plants might tell us something about the auxin relationships and other physiological conditions that prevail during leaf expansion. Interpreted with due caution in this way, plant anatomy could present for us a permanent record of preceding biochemical events— once we have learned adequately to read the code.

FIBRES

Although fibres vary considerably in length, they are typically many times longer than broad. Most fibres are elongated elements with pointed tips, a narrow lumen and thick secondary walls.

Fibres may occur in roots, stems, leaves and fruits, in association with a number of different tissues. They may be present in the xylem or phloem, as a sheath or bundle cap associated with the vascular bundles, especially in leaves, or in the parenchymatous tissues of the pith or cortex. Fibres may occur singly or, more commonly, in bundles. They are sometimes classified[91] in two groups: xylem fibres, and extra-xylary fibres, the latter including all those fibres which occur in tissues other than the xylem, i.e. phloem, cortical and perivascular fibres.

In monocotyledonous leaves fibres may be present not only as a sheath around the vascular bundles but also extending between the bundles and the upper and lower epidermis. It is whole strands of this kind which constitute the 'hard' or leaf fibres used commercially, e.g. sisal (*Agave sisalana*); 'soft' fibres, e.g. flax (*Linum usitatissimum*), are mainly phloem fibres.

Origin and development

Fibres may originate from the procambium or vascular cambium, if they are associated with the primary or secondary xylem or phloem, or from the ground meristem. In the stem of *Linum*, for example, the protophloem comprises a mixture of large and small cells. The large cells are young fibres, the small ones the sieve tubes and companion cells of the phloem.[86] These fibres continue to enlarge and are the source of flax. The fibres of hemp, *Cannabis sativa*,[156] and of ramie, *Boehmeria nivea*,[157] also develop among functional phloem elements from procambial cells.

Primary fibres grow in length with the organ in which they occur. The fibres of *Cannabis* (hemp) and *Corchorus* (jute) extend as the internodes of the stem elongate, but may continue to increase in length after the period of internodal extension.[156] This is true also of the fibres in the fruit of *Luffa*;[225] these networks of fibres are used commercially as sponges. In *Boehmeria*, the fibres elongate faster than the surrounding cells, and at the same time deposition of wall thickening begins at the basal end of the cells.[157] Individual fibres may attain considerable—not to say striking —lengths, e.g. 1–10 cm in hemp, and up to 55 cm in ramie.[2]

The fibres of ramie continue to elongate over a period of months, and may finally attain an increase in length of the order of $2\frac{1}{2}$ million per cent.[116] These cells are thus in a different way no less remarkable than sclereids. Deposition of the secondary wall takes place after elongation of the fibre has ceased. In *Boehmeria*, the basal end of a fibre may have a thick secondary wall while the apical end still has living contents and a thin wall.[157] Some fibres are septate, with thin transverse walls, e.g. *Vitis, Zingiber* (Fig. 6.7);

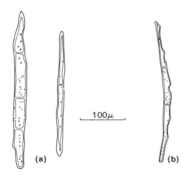

Fig. 6.7   Septate fibres of (a) *Vitis* and (b) *Zingiber.* ×115.

in such fibres the protoplast may remain living for a long time. These thin transverse septa may be formed after the deposition of the secondary wall material on the longitudinal wall of the fibre. Fibres are usually defined as cells which have no living contents at maturity, but recent evidence[107] indicates that xylem fibres, at least, may in fact retain living contents for several years. Fibres may show slight indentations in the wall due to pressure against neighbouring files of parenchyma cells (Fig. 6.7b). Flax fibres, which may have 90% of the cross-sectional area occupied by the thick wall, are cellulosic, but the walls of many fibres are lignified. Pits are often present in the fibre wall; some of these may be cross pits, i.e. pits with crossed apertures.

Economic uses

Fibres produced by plants have been put to economic use for many centuries. There is evidence that cotton was used between 7200 and 5200 B.C. in the Tehuacán Valley of Mexico;[171] cotton is obtained from hairs on the seed coat, however, and is not a true fibre in the botanical sense (see Chapter 7). About 10,000 years ago the desert peoples of Utah, U.S.A., knew both how to extract plant fibres, perhaps by chewing the plant parts, and how to fashion them into cord; cordage of various kinds has been found in caves at levels dated from 9201 B.C. onwards.[145,231] A complete string bag or net made of the knotted fibres of *Apocynum* has been dated at about 5000 B.C. There is evidence that flax and hemp have been cultivated for fibre for 4,000 or 5,000 years.[14,116]

At the present time plants from 44 different families are used as sources of fibre. Common commercial fibres may be divided into textile fibres, including flax (*Linum usitatissimum*), jute (*Corchorus* spp.), hemp (*Cannabis sativa*), and ramie (*Boehmeria nivea*), and cordage fibres, including sisal (*Agave sisalana*), bowstring hemp (*Sansevieria* spp.), and New Zealand hemp (*Phormium tenax*). Extraction of most fibres is carried out by a process known as 'retting'. This involves a release of fibres from surrounding tissues by bacterial decomposition of the middle lamellae between the cells. The tissues are left in water for a considerable time while this takes place. Then the retted stems are dried and passed between rollers, which separates the fibres from the other tissues. Finally they are combed, beaten out and placed in bales.[57]

Factors controlling differentiation

Despite the importance of plant fibres, an understanding of what controls or affects their differentiation is largely lacking, though it has long been known that physical stress can stimulate their development. For example, tendrils of *Cyclanthera* which were attached to a support contained more fibres than did tendrils of the same age that were not attached to a support, and the fibres also had thicker walls.[129] In *Cannabis sativa*, the fibres were found to be much stronger in plants from well-watered soil. The physiological factors underlying these observations remain to be investigated. Indeed, the answers to many questions concerning the formation and development of fibres have still to be sought: for example, what factors control their differentiation, not from one, but from several different tissues, what controls the elongation of fibres, and what affects their thickness and strength. Even in the era of man-made fibres, many plant fibres remain economically important and some of these questions would seem to have economic, and perhaps also agronomic, implications. Recent studies of the effects of gibberellic acid (GA) on fibre development constitute an interesting attempt to investigate these matters, which may have some economic importance. In jute, treatment with GA increased the amount and percentage of fibre per plant;[229] in jute and hemp, individual fibres of treated plants were considerably longer, wider and more thick-walled.[15,242] The length of the bundles of fibres which constitute the commercial fibre was increased up to four-fold in GA-treated plants of several species.[241] Interesting as these results are, however, there is still plenty of scope for work in this field.

7

Epidermis

The epidermis is the outermost layer or layers of cells on all plant parts during primary growth. It is thus in direct contact with the environment and, as might perhaps be expected, is subject to structural modification by various environmental factors. Both because of its relationships with the environment and because of the conspicuous differentiation that often occurs among the cells of this layer, the epidermis is an interesting tissue and has been much studied. The structure of the epidermis has been fully described by Linsbauer.[166]

The epidermis of the stem, leaves and floral parts originates from the surface layer of the shoot apical meristem (see Part 2, Chapter 3). That of the root originates from a layer of cells in the root apical meristem that is covered by the root cap; in different species, the epidermis may have a common origin with the cortex or with the root cap (see Part 2, Chapter 2). Usually the epidermis consists of only one layer of cells, but in a few species the cells of this layer may divide periclinally to give rise to a several-layered, or multiple, epidermis. Such a tissue occurs in the aerial roots of some species and is called the velamen. A multiple epidermis also occurs in the leaves of some plants, e.g. species of Moraceae, Piperaceae.

The epidermis of both root and shoot may be differentiated into various kinds of cells. In both instances epidermal cells may elongate at an angle to the surface of the organ to give rise to hairs. In the epidermis of the leaf, and often also of the stem, stomata may be present; in some species cork cells and cells containing silica are also differentiated. Some epidermal cells, or even hairs, may also contain crystals, for example the lithocysts in which cysto-liths are formed in the epidermis of *Ficus* (Fig. 3.10). Since these different structures originate from single cells and in a (usually) single-layered tissue which is relatively easy to observe, the epidermis has been used in many studies of cell differentiation and its controlling factors. At least the early stages of differentiation in the root, stem and leaf epidermis are remarkably similar.

The epidermis may persist during the life of the plant or, in species which undergo secondary growth, it may be sloughed off along with underlying tissues after the formation of the periderm.

ROOT

In the epidermis of the roots of many flowering plants some of the cells give rise to root hairs. These are merely projections of the epidermal cell, except in isolated instances where multicellular root hairs have been observed.

For a short distance (about 100 μ) behind the tip of the root all the epidermal cells divide and there is little or no evidence of differentiation. Between 100 and 275 μ from the root tip the probability that an epidermal cell will divide becomes progressively less.[83]

Root hairs first grow out at some little distance behind the tip of the root; this distance varies in different species and in the same species under different conditions. In some roots those cells which give rise to root hairs, which are called trichoblasts, are morphologically distinct from those which do not; in other species all epidermal cells are morphologically similar, but only some of them form root hairs. Apparently there is a relationship between length of cell and outgrowth of hair, the shortest cells developing the longest hairs. This suggests that the outgrowth of a root hair indicates, in part, a change in the direction of growth of the cell.[62,63]

Root hairs are generally considered to function by increasing the absorptive surface of the plant. Certainly the area over which absorption could occur is greatly enhanced where root hairs are present. However, it has recently been shown that the rate of influx of water through the hairless epidermal surface is similar to that through root hairs, and, further, that short hairs are actually more efficient in absorption than long ones.[209] The needs of the plant could be satisfied either by only a few of the root hairs actually present, or by only a proportion of their surface area, and it seems likely that the main biological advantage of root hairs is that by means of their lateral extension they can come into contact with otherwise untapped sources of water.[209] Many aquatic plants possess well developed root hairs, but in others, e.g. *Elodea*, root hairs are formed only, or principally, when the plant grows in soil or mud.[61,284] When grown in water in total darkness *Elodea* produced root hairs, and this was attributed to lack of cuticle, which was present in roots grown in the light and might have acted as a mechanical barrier to outgrowth of hairs. On the other hand, if CO_2 was bubbled through the nutrient medium root hairs were formed on roots grown in light, and a fatty layer did develop on the epidermis. This was shown not to be a true cuticle, however, the CO_2 having prevented the oxidation of the fats to form a cuticle.[73]

A thin cuticle normally covers the cell wall of the root hair, and mucilage may occur superficially.[74] The extreme tip of the root hair is probably the main site of synthesis of cellulose, although work with the isotope ^{14}C indicates that synthesis occurs over a length of about 120 μ behind the tip.[24] Electron microscopy indicates that the epidermal cell wall consists of two parts, an inner densely staining region and a much wider outer zone. Apparently the root hair represents an outgrowth of the inner region only. Both the root hairs and other epidermal cells contain many vesicles associated with the dictyosomes; these vesicles are much larger than in cells from other parts of the root.[163]

Trichoblasts

In some species, notably many grasses, the cells of the epidermis that will give rise to root hairs (trichoblasts) are distinguished in various ways from the other epidermal cells. They are usually smaller and have dense cytoplasm. An interesting example is found in the roots of the aquatic plant *Hydrocharis morsus-ranae*, in which the trichoblasts are easily distinguishable from adjacent epidermal cells by their dense cytoplasm (Fig. 7.1) and other features. For example, in roots grown in the light well developed chloroplasts with grana are present in all epidermal cells except the trichoblasts, in which the chloroplasts progressively revert.[254] In other species, e.g. *Sinapis alba*, white mustard, certain longitudinal files of cells give rise to root hairs. A considerable amount of work has been carried out on the differentiation of trichoblasts, including studies of changes in histochemistry and fine structure.

In some plants, including grasses, the trichoblasts are formed by unequal division of an epidermal cell, preceded by an unequal distribution of cytoplasm. The cytoplasm becomes concentrated at the apical end of the cell (i.e. the end towards the root apex) and later the cell divides to form a small cell in this position and a larger cell proximally. Avers[18] has pointed out that the mitosis itself is asymmetric, and is not merely a symmetrical process occurring in an asymmetrical position at one end of the cell. Thus not merely the distribution of the cytoplasm, but also the mitotic figure itself is asymmetric in these cells. Interesting observations on the roots of species of *Potamogeton* indicate that the trichoblasts may induce the formation of short, densely cytoplasmic cells in the underlying tissues. Some distance from the root tip, in a region where neighbouring cells no longer undergo much division, an equal division occurs in the cells underlying

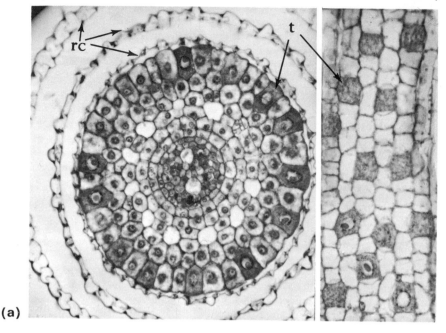

Fig. 7.1 Trichoblasts (t) in the root epidermis of *Hydrocharis morsus-ranae.* (a) Transverse section of root, showing the densely cytoplasmic trichoblasts, which also have larger nuclei and nucleoli than adjoining epidermal cells. A three-layered root cap (rc) is present. × 200. (b) Tangential longitudinal section through the epidermis, showing the densely cytoplasmic trichoblasts. × 200.

the trichoblasts; the resulting cells divide again, forming a row of short, densely cytoplasmic cells.[258]

In species without distinctive trichoblasts the cytoplasm is more or less uniformly distributed and approximately equal division of the cell follows.[224] The proportion of cells that differentiate as trichoblasts is fairly constant under different conditions, but the number of these cells that actually give rise to root hairs is variable.[284] It seems that the factors that control the outgrowth of trichoblasts may not be identical with those that lead to their formation. This is, of course, a common phenomenon in morphogenesis. The growth rate of trichoblasts is less than that of other epidermal cells in a region of the root just proximal to the apex[63]; the size relationship between the trichoblasts and other epidermal cells may change during growth (Fig. 7.2).

It is obviously important to establish what distinctive physiological and morphological differences exist between trichoblasts and ordinary epidermal cells. By this means it may be possible to discover the factors that

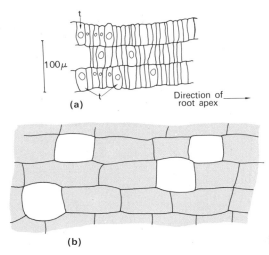

Fig. 7.2 Trichoblasts in the root epidermis of *Hydrocharis morsus-ranae*. (a) Near the tip of the root. The trichoblasts (t) are larger than the other cells of the epidermis and have larger nuclei.(b) Just distal to the region of emergence of root hairs. Ordinary epidermal cells (stippled) contain numerous chloroplasts; the trichoblasts are rich in cytoplasm but contain no plastids visible with the ight microscope. × 155.

are important in affecting or controlling their ultimate destiny. Early workers suggested that materials that would stimulate root hair formation moved in a polar manner in the root, accumulating at the apical (i.e. distal) end of the cells.[224] Both nuclear and cytoplasmic differences are, indeed, now known to exist between the trichoblasts and other adjacent cells of the epidermis. In the discussion which follows, those cells of the developing epidermis which will not give rise to root hairs will be termed hairless initials, as opposed to the trichoblasts or hair initials. In *Hydrocharis* the amount of DNA in the nuclei of the trichoblasts increases with distance from the root tip up to a value approximately eight times that in adjacent cells.[70] In grasses which possess distinctive trichoblasts nucleolar volume is greater in these than in other epidermal cells (Fig. 7.3).[169,210] In two species without trichoblasts there was also a difference in nucleolar size—though a less clear-cut one—between those cells which give rise to root hairs and hairless cells.[210] Differences in nucleolar size could also be detected in younger epidermal cells which were not yet differentiated. Recent observations indicate also that in grasses lacking distinctive trichoblasts hairs are formed from cells which not only have larger nucleoli but also a greater concentration of protein bodies than the hairless cells adjacent to them.[211] Thus cytological differences may be detectable between cells with different destinies even when morphological differences are not evident.

Intense staining of RNA and ribonucleoprotein was observed in trichoblasts of *Phleum* between 150 and 300 µ from the root apex.[169] Trichoblasts are also the sites of the differential activity of several enzymes. By the use

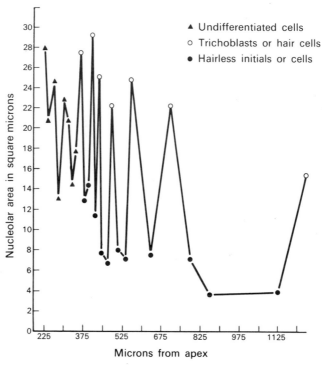

▲ Undifferentiated cells

○ Trichoblasts or hair cells

● Hairless initials or cells

Nucleolar area in square microns

Microns from apex

Fig. 7.3   Nucleolar areas of 26 cells in sequence making up a row in the root epidermis of *Festuca arundinacea*. The root was stained with acetocarmine. (From Rothwell,[210] Fig. 8, p. 175.)

of stains that are specific for certain enzymes it is possible to establish the relative distribution of the enzymes in the cells of a particular tissue, a technique of considerable value in studies of differentiation. Using this technique it was found that both cytochrome oxidase and acid phosphatase occur at a high level in the trichoblasts at an early stage of differentiation (Fig. 7.4).[16,19] In festucoid grasses, which possess trichoblasts in their roots, intensified activity of the enzyme acid phosphatase in the trichoblasts and loss of activity in the hairless initial cells was evident before full development of these cells. In panicoid grasses, which have no distinctive trichoblasts, no cells inactive in phosphatase were evident during differentiation.[19]

Fig. 7.4 Activity of the enzyme 5-nucleotidase in root epidermal cells of *Phleum*, after histochemical treatment. Active trichoblasts (darkly stained) alternate with inactive hairless initials. × 200. (From Avers,[17] Fig. 8, p. 141.)

More recent work on enzyme activity in epidermal cells of grass roots has revealed an added complexity. It now appears that the activity of enzymes, in this case phosphatases, in the hairless or hair cell initials differs according to the position of these cells along the root. In the cells within 100 μ from the apex of the root little differentiation of the cells was observed; in the region 100–200 μ behind the tip the hairless initials usually showed phosphatase activity while the trichoblasts did not; and from about 200–300 μ behind the root apex the trichoblasts, in general, were active and the hairless initials were not.[72] It thus appears that, superimposed upon differences between future hair-initiating and hairless cells, there are other effects produced by the general gradient of differentiation along the root. It seems possible that this may be related in some way to the progressive differentiation of underlying tissues, which is, of course, proceeding quite rapidly in a basipetal direction. As discussed in Chapter 2, the nature of the underlying tissues may affect the differentiation of the superficial layer in particular regions.

In interpreting these interesting observations on enzyme activity in the trichoblasts and hairless initials, emphasis is usually placed on the positive, and thus more evident, changes that take place in the trichoblasts. For example, it is considered that high levels of certain enzymes may be necessary for root hair formation. However, to the present writer these observations suggest rather that the *loss* of phosphatase activity (or some other

4

change of which this is a symptom) may be important in *restricting* the potentiality for root hair development. Observations on the fine structure of differentiating epidermal cells,[18] which have seemed difficult to interpret, also appear compatible with this viewpoint: namely, that the *restriction* of developmental potentialities may be at least as important in differentiation as the acquisition of positive features such as high enzyme activity. It seems logical to consider the possibility that even in species with trichoblasts all cells are initially capable of giving rise to root hairs; at this early stage of development they are also all rich in enzymes. During differentiation some cells show less enzyme activity, and also lose the capacity to form hairs.

In the roots of some species trichoblasts do not alternate in the longitudinal plane with hairless initials, but form whole rows running longitudinally along the root, other longitudinal rows being composed of hairless initials. The trichoblasts may then have a particular spatial relationship with underlying tissues. For example, in the roots of *Sinapis alba*, the trichoblasts are aligned with the radiating rows of anticlinal walls of cortical cells and the intervening intercellular spaces (Fig. 7.5). Because of

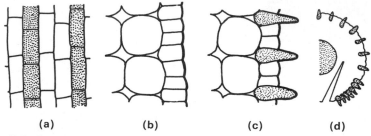

| (a) | (b) | (c) | (d) |

Fig. 7.5 Trichoblasts. (a) Distribution of trichoblasts (dotted) and ordinary cells in the epidermis of the roots of some dicotyledons. (b) Transverse section showing part of the epidermis and cortex before differentiation. (c) Position of emerging root hairs. (d) The effect of an incision between the vascular cylinder and the epidermis. All epidermal cells are giving rise to root hairs. (From Bünning,[40] Fig. 4, (IV), p. 115.)

this spatial relationship, transport to the trichoblasts of substances from the vascular cylinder and inner layers of the cortex, which are still meristematic and densely protoplasmic at this level, will evidently differ from that to the other epidermal cells. Some authors[62] argue that substances are more readily transported to the trichoblasts through the intercellular spaces than to other epidermal cells through the cells of the cortex; others maintain that the trichoblasts are, in fact, somewhat isolated physiologically from the central tissues of the root. This latter interpretation is supported by the results of experiments in which the epidermis was separated from the inner tissues by an incision; after this treatment all the isolated epidermal cells, when adequately nourished, gave rise to root hairs (Fig. 7.5d).[40] Possibly an inhibitor may be radially transported from the central region of the root of some species through the cortical cells to the epidermis, the potential trichoblasts escaping its effects by virtue of their position. Such an interpretation would again place some emphasis on the importance of the restrictive changes taking place in those cells which fail to give rise to root hairs.

AERIAL PARTS

The epidermis of the aerial parts of the plant consists of cells which are more or less tabular in shape, or else with much convoluted anticlinal walls (those at right angles to the surface) (Fig. 7.6). In the leaf the cells of the

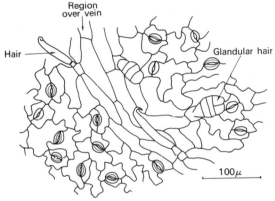

Fig. 7.6 Lower epidermis of the leaf of *Phaseolus vulgaris*, showing two kinds of hair, slightly raised guard cells of stomata, and convolute epidermal cells (except over the veins). × 155.

abaxial (lower) epidermis are often more lobed than those of the adaxial (upper) epidermis. There are usually few intercellular spaces, or none. In photosynthetic organs such as leaves and young stems the epidermal cells are normally devoid of fully developed chloroplasts, except for the guard cells of the stomata. These are paired cells which surround a pore in the epidermis through which gaseous exchange, including the movement of water vapour, takes place. Epidermal cells are usually thin-walled, but in some species, especially among gymnosperms, they may be thick-walled and even lignified. Pigments, e.g. anthocyanin, may be present in epidermal cells.

Cuticle

Very often a layer of fatty material, or cutin, is deposited on the surface of the epidermal cell wall, forming the cuticle. This substance is impervious to water, and may have a protective function. When the cuticle is of considerable thickness, its chemical nature often varies in different layers, at least proportionally, and may include cutin and wax. The innermost layers may lack cutin, and the outermost may lack cellulose, various proportions of these substances being present in intervening regions.[238] The cuticle is extremely resistant to micro-organisms. Thus in the living plant it affords some protection, perhaps largely mechanical, against infection by pathogens, and in fossilized plant remains it may be extremely well preserved, being resistant to decay. It may persist for millions of years, and can be isolated fairly readily from fossils and studied; indeed, fossil plants can very often be successfully identified in this way.[133]

Distinctive cuticular patterns often preserve many of the characteristic features of the underlying epidermis, for example type of stomata and hairs, and their distribution. This may be useful not only in identification of fossils, but in recognizing small fragments of plants, as is necessary, for example, in pharmacognosy, forensic medicine, and studies in animal nutrition. In one investigation 16 species of plants eaten by hill sheep were identified from cuticular fragments in the rumen and faeces, whereas others had been completely digested or were otherwise unrecognizable.[177]

In many plants conspicuous deposits of wax are formed on the surface of the cuticle. It is this wax which gives the 'bloom' to some fruits, e.g. grapes, and to glaucous leaves. When viewed under the electron microscope, the wax is seen to form many projections and folds, and by the carbon replica technique complex wax patterns from the surface of the epidermis can be studied. This technique is used mainly for materials which are opaque to electrons, and depends on depositing a replicating material, such as carbon, on the specimen. The replica, which consists of a thin film of electron-transparent material, is then removed and examined under the microscope. The wax patterns vary in different species, and to some extent within a single species under different conditions. Wax formation apparently begins at an early stage in leaf development and persists until a late one; the projections seem to reach a fairly uniform density and height and then remain relatively unchanged.[149] The problem of how the wax reaches the leaf surface, after it is secreted by the cell, is controversial. Some workers maintain that numerous plasmodesmata, called ectodesmata, are present in the outer walls of epidermal cells;[118] others have been quite unable to find pores of any kind through which the wax could have been extruded.[149,214] On the basis of a recent study using the freeze-etch technique of electron microscopy the existence of microchannels through which the wax is transported is again claimed.[130]

These wax patterns on the surface of the epidermis are extremely important in that they affect the degree to which the surface can be wetted. Surface wax resists wetting by sprays, etc., much better than a smooth cuticle.[214] Thus the degree of susceptibility of a plant to herbicides, or the effectiveness of a fungicide, may depend on the extent of development of this surface wax; the selective action of herbicides may be due in part to the amount of surface wax in different species. The development of wax is affected by light, being greater at high light intensities. It has also been noted that a thicker layer of wax is formed in plants which are grown slowly.[149] Thus various environmental factors can affect wax formation, and hence the reaction to various spraying treatments.

Wax formed by plants may be commercially useful if it is produced in sufficient quantity. The wax deposited on the leaves of the wax palm, *Copernicia cerifera*, is called carnauba wax and is used in the manufacture of phonograph records and various polishes. Only about 6 ounces of wax are obtained from 50 of the large palm leaves.[22]

Hairs

A hair or trichome is formed by the outgrowth of an epidermal cell. Plant hairs have been described in detail by Uphof.[261] They are formed on all parts of the plant, including stamens, e.g. *Tradescantia*, and seeds, e.g. *Gossypium*, cotton (Fig. 7.7). Cell division may take place, so that the hair becomes multicellular, or it may remain unicellular. Multicellular hairs may consist of a single row of cells, or of many rows. Trichomes are sometimes classified as either glandular hairs, which have a secretory function, or covering hairs, which do not. Scales consist of a discoid plate of cells, usually on a short stalk. Certain leaves, e.g. *Olea*, *Hippophaë*, have a dense covering of scales on the abaxial surface. Scales, like hairs, apparently originate from a single cell. Covering hairs may occur in tufts, as in the leaf of *Hamamelis*, or they may be complex branching structures, as in *Verbascum* (Fig. 7.8). The epidermal cells of many petals have small hair-like projections known as papillae.

Either unicellular or multicellular hairs may be glandular. In such hairs there is a stalk and a head, the head being the secretory region. A cuticle-like structure covers the cell(s) of the head, and the secretion accumulates in the sac formed between the cell or cells and the cuticle (Fig. 7.8d). Oils, resins and camphors may be secreted in this way. Peppermint (*Mentha piperita*) has hairs of this type; they are formed at an early stage in leaf development.[138]

The cell walls of most trichomes are usually thin and cellulosic, but some hairs have lignified cell walls, e.g. those on the seed-coat of *Strychnos nux-vomica*, the source of strychnine. The unicellular hairs on the seed-coat of *Gossypium*, which are cellulosic, are the source of cotton, and are of great commercial importance. In early stages of development the hairs are visible as slight outgrowths from the seed-coat (Fig. 7.7), but in some varieties they may be ultimately 2 in. long. These hairs have been utilized by man

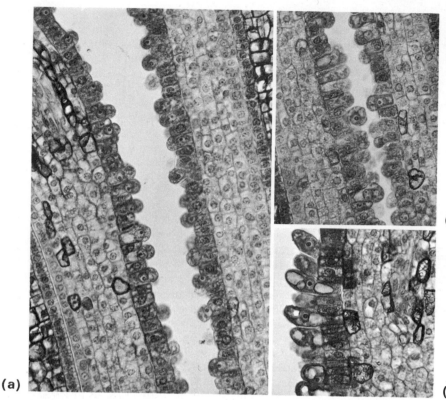

(a)   (b)   (c)

Fig. 7.7 Transverse section of young developing ovules of *Gossypium hirsutum* (cotton) showing early stages in the development of the unicellular hairs (commercial cotton) from the testa. In (a) and (b) the edges of two adjacent ovules in the ovary are shown. (a) Very young stage, with hairs just growing out; (b) slightly later stage; (c) later stage, hairs becoming vacuolate.   × 300.

for some 7,000 or 8,000 years, and fabrics woven from cotton are known from 900–200 B.C.[171] The growing of cotton is an important industry in parts of America and Africa, and the economy of the great industrial areas of Lancashire, England, which have a damp climate particularly suitable for cotton spinning, depended for many years on the manufacture of cotton fabrics. The Lancashire cotton industry was built up in the fifteenth and sixteenth centuries and prospered until it encountered serious competition from man-made fibres in more recent times. The industrial and economic importance of this plant structure needs no further emphasis. The hairs on the seed-coat of *Ceiba pentandra*, the source of kapok, are also of commercial importance.

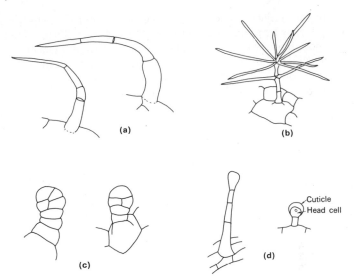

Fig. 7.8 Covering and glandular trichomes. (a) Uniseriate covering trichomes from the leaf of *Lycopersicon*. (b) Branched covering trichomes from the leaf of *Verbascum*. (c) Glandular trichomes with multicellular heads from the leaf of *Cucurbita*. (d) Glandular trichomes with unicellular heads from the leaf of *Pelargonium*. (a), (b) and (d) ×115. (c) ×180.

Trichomes are usually of a characteristic form within a species, and may be of taxonomic significance. For example, the numerous species of *Rhododendron*[64] and of the Oleaceae can be identified at least to some extent by their trichomes. Carlquist[48] has emphasized the importance in taxonomic work of considering all the trichomes present; he calls this the 'trichome complement' of the plant.

The function of non-glandular trichomes in the plant is obscure, though it is often thought that they are protective and may prevent undue water loss. This view may be attributable to the prevalence of hairs on species from dry habitats. Some recent work is interesting in this connection. If the inhibition of axillary bud growth on isolated segments of pea stems was maintained by applied auxin, and especially if this inhibition was then partially released, there was a conspicuous outgrowth of two kinds of trichomes on the leaves of the buds. No trichomes were present on buds after more complete release of bud inhibition by treatment with kinetin. Also, trichomes were formed abundantly on buds of intact etiolated plants that had been grown for 30 days with a limited water supply. In various other instances it was found that the development of trichomes on pea leaves coincided with some imperfection of the transpiration stream, sometimes caused by incomplete contact between basipetally and acropetally differentiating xylem or by partial destruction of this tissue.[233] These observations are the more interesting in that hairs of this kind are not usually found on pea leaves. Such findings seem to suggest that trichomes may be formed in response to some water deficit (though since they occur in some aquatic plants (Fig. 10.1) this cannot be the complete explanation); whether in fact they protect the plant to an important extent against further water loss remains uncertain. The functions of numerous plant structures, often assigned to them many years ago and cited ever since, are still imperfectly understood and are deserving of further study with modern methods. Sometimes a relationship of a different kind is revealed, just as in this instance there appears to be a causal relationship, rather than a functional one, between limitation of water supply and the presence of trichomes. There is scope for much further observation and experiment in this field.

Stomata

Stomata (singular, stoma) occur on most of the aerial parts of plants, though predominantly on leaves and young stems. A stoma consists of a pore surrounded by two *guard cells*. The epidermal cells adjoining the guard cells often differ in size or arrangement from the rest of the epidermal cells; such cells are called *subsidiary cells*. The stoma, together with the subsidiary cells, is sometimes termed the stomatal complex. In grasses, at least, the subsidiary cells are separated from the guard cells by a thin wall devoid of plasmodesmata or pits.[39] The guard cells usually contain chloroplasts, though electron microscopy indicates that these contain fewer and less well organized lamellae than the chloroplasts of mesophyll cells, resembling early stages in development of normal chloroplasts.[39] However, chlorophyll is present and active assimilation apparently takes place in the guard cells.[289] In some species the guard cells may also differ from the other cells of the epidermis in lacking pigments, or crystals or protein bodies.[293] In most dicotyledons the guard cells are somewhat kidney-shaped, having localized ledges or projections of thick wall or cuticle. In many monocotyledons they are dumb-bell shaped, having a narrow central region with a thick wall and narrow lumen (Fig. 7.9). This thick-walled region is thought to be important in the mechanism for opening and closing the pore, which is of course of great functional importance, and guard cells of this kind have been compared to a balloon with masking tape along one side.[293] On inflation, such a structure would swell at the two ends, which are thin-walled (or devoid of tape); this swelling would result in the concave bending of the thick-walled (taped) central region. When two adjacent cells act in this way, the pore between the central thick-walled regions would be caused to open.

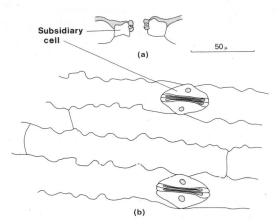

Fig. 7.9 Stomata from *Zea mays*. (a) Transverse section of leaf, showing thickened guard cells and subsidiary cells. (b) Paradermal section of the leaf, showing guard cells, subsidiary cells and other epidermal cells in surface view. Nuclei (dotted) of guard cells are much elongated through the narrow part of the cell. Thick walled regions are stippled. × 345.

In leaves stomata may occur on both surfaces, or on only one. In most mesophytic plants, i.e. those in a temperate climate with an adequate water supply, stomata are more frequent on the abaxial surface. In aquatic plants stomata may be absent or, in floating leaves, restricted to the upper or adaxial surface. In many xerophytes, i.e. plants which usually have a restricted water supply, the stomata may be deeply sunken below the level of the other epidermal cells, or restricted to grooves or cavities in the leaf surface. In most parallel-veined leaves the stomata occur in rows parallel to the long axis of the leaf, and are formed from apex to base; in most net-veined leaves they are scattered over the leaf surface, and new stomata may be formed between existing ones. A value known as the stomatal index can be readily calculated.

$$\text{Stomatal index} = \frac{\text{No. of stomata}}{\text{No. of stomata} + \text{No. of epidermal cells}} \times 100$$

where the numbers of stomata and of ordinary epidermal cells are measured within a unit area. This value is found to be reasonably constant for any particular species, being affected to any great extent only by humidity. Both the size and frequency of stomata are affected also by the degree of ploidy of the plant.[213] In polyploid plants the stomata are larger and less frequent per unit area of leaf.

It is evident from the foregoing that the guard cells are idioblasts, differing in various ways from the surrounding epidermal cells. The distinctive nature of the guard cell mother cell, or initial cell, is evident not only in developing leaf blades but also in stems and petioles.[152,180] For example, in the developing petiole of *Populus* the guard cell mother cell shows an ability to synthesize starch, and other distinctive features, at an early stage of development.[180]

Stomata in dicotyledons may originate by a division resulting in an oblique wall in an epidermal cell.[198] The smaller cell resulting from this division functions as the guard cell mother cell. In many monocotyledons the guard cell mother cell is formed by an asymmetric division of an epidermal cell; the process is similar to the formation of some trichoblasts in the root epidermis. A differential distribution of cytoplasm first takes place, the cytoplasm accumulating at the apical, or distal, end of the cells. Subsequently the cell divides asymmetrically, and the distal small, densely cytoplasmic cell functions as the guard cell mother cell.[41,43] In the leaves[243] and stems[152] of grasses the small idioblast thus formed may give rise to a hair, a pair of guard cells, or a silica cell plus a suberous (cork) cell; its final development depends in part, at least, on its position in the epidermis. Because of the divergent fates of their products, these small cells are of great interest in studies of differentiation.

In some monocotyledons the guard cell mother cell induces divisions in the adjacent epidermal cells, probably in part by setting up an osmotic gradient. The smaller cells produced from these induced asymmetric divisions in the adjoining epidermal cells constitute the subsidiary cells.[244,246] After the formation of the subsidiary cells the guard cell mother cell divides by a wall parallel to the long axis of the leaf to give rise to the two guard cells. Temperature changes have differential effects on the division of the guard cell mother cells and on the preceding formation of the subsidiary cells by induced mitoses, suggesting that these are quite distinct processes.[6]

Experiments on stomata

A number of experiments have been carried out in an endeavour to discover the factors controlling stomatal formation and distribution. Bünning and Biegert[43] showed that after centrifugation the normal accumulation of cytoplasm at and the movement of the nucleus towards the apical pole of the epidermal cells of onion leaves (*Allium cepa*) was altered, and an initial-like cell was formed at the basal (proximal) pole instead (Fig. 7.10). This did not, however, give rise to guard cells.

This experiment interfered with the distribution of the cytoplasm in differentiating cells. Treatments affecting the nucleus also gave some interesting results. For example, in barley seedlings treated with 2-mer-

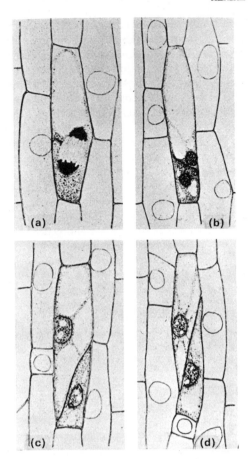

Fig. 7.10 The effect of centrifugation on stomatal development in *Allium cepa*. A stomatal mother cell is apparently formed at the basal cell pole. (a) Displacement of the nuclear spindle after centrifugation. (b) Cell wall formation in the basal part of the cell after centrifuging for 3 hours. (c) Outgrowth of the cell formed towards the base, 12 hours after the end of centrifugation. (d) The same, 24 hours after the end of centrifugation. (From Bünning,[41] Fig. 23, p. 23, after Bünning and Biegert.)

captoethanol, a substance that interferes with spindle formation, a large number of stomata had one subsidiary cell missing.[246] This substance blocks mitosis temporarily, and after growth is resumed some guard cell mother cells divide by a wall perpendicular to the long axis of the leaf, i.e. at right angles to the normal. Similar results were obtained by simply removing the sheaths of culm leaves from the plant, without further treatment. In such leaves mitoses occurred again in guard cell mother cells after a period of quiescence consequent upon removal of the leaf; about 88% of such mitoses produced guard cells abnormally oriented at right angles to the long axis of the leaf.[243] The effects that these treatments have in common are a temporary delay in the onset of mitosis and the frequent absence of subsidiary cells as well as the reorientation of mitoses in the guard cell mother cells. Before mitosis the latter synthesize both DNA and RNA very actively.[247]

Working with the leaves of various dicotyledons, Bünning and Sagromsky[44] showed that treatment of developing leaves with alkali stimulated the formation of stomata, whereas treatment with acid was inhibitory. One half of a young leaf was treated, while the other half was left untreated and served as the control. Treatment with the hormone indoleacetic acid stimulated cell division but inhibited formation of stomata, suggesting that the production of such a substance by stomata and other meristemoids might be, or might resemble, the normal mechanism by which the formation of other similar structures in their immediate vicinity is prevented (see Chapter 2). Wounding the leaf also inhibited stomatal development in proximity to the wound. Treatment with extracts of growing tissues was also tried. For example, when a paste consisting of the tissues of young pods which were forming stomata was smeared on the leaves of *Theobroma cacao*, stomatal development in the leaves was completely prevented.[44] Experiments of this kind seem worth pursuing with modern more precise techniques.

Types of Stomata

In most species the number and arrangement of the subsidiary cells around the stomata are relatively constant. Various classifications of stomata according to these arrangements have been drawn up, and are sometimes useful to taxonomists. Not all the stomata present on a leaf are good examples of a single type, and fairly large numbers of stomata should be examined to determine the most prevalent type. The early classifications were based on mature structure only, but it is now believed that ontogenetic studies of stomatal development are important.

Solereder[232] described four types of stomatal complex that occurred especially in certain families of dicotyledons, and to which he gave family names, i.e. Ranunculaceous, Cruciferous, Rubiaceous, and Caryophyllaceous. Metcalfe and Chalk[179] gave rather more descriptive names to these types, as follows:

Anomocytic or irregular-celled: the surrounding cells are indefinite in number and do not differ from the other epidermal cells (Fig. 7.11a);

Anisocytic or unequal-celled: usually three subsidiary cells surround the stoma, one cell being considerably smaller or larger than the other two (Fig. 7.11b);

Diacytic or cross-celled: two subsidiary cells surround the stoma with their common wall at right angles to the guard cells (Fig. 7.11c);

Paracytic or parallel-celled: one or more (often two) subsidiary cells are present, with their long axes parallel to the guard cells (Fig. 7.11d).

In addition to these types, two others are sometimes recognized: *actinocytic*, with four or more subsidiary cells elongated radially to the stoma, and *cyclocytic*, with four or more subsidiary cells arranged in a narrow ring round the stoma.[238]

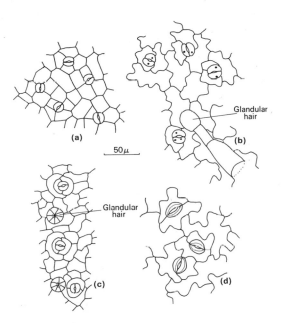

Fig. 7.11 Types of stomata of dicotyledonous plants. (a) Anomocytic, having no special subsidiary cells (*Cucurbita*); (b) anisocytic, having 3 subsidiary cells, one larger or smaller than the other two (*Petunia*); (c) diacytic, having 2 subsidiary cells with their common wall at right angles to the guard cells (*Hygrophila*); (d) paracytic, having 2 subsidiary cells with their long axes parallel to the guard cells (*Phaseolus*). ×180.

This classification takes no account of the ontogeny of the stomata, and it is known that the various types can be arrived at by different developmental paths. Relatively minor anomalies during ontogeny, such as fewer mitotic divisions or a slight difference in the position of the cell wall, can result in formation on the same leaf of stomata of different types.[197] Accordingly, a new type of classification based on ontogeny has recently been proposed.[196] Stomata are divided into the following types:

Mesogenous: the subsidiary cells have a common origin with the guard cells, developing from the same meristemoid as the guard cells;

Perigenous: the subsidiary cells do not have a common origin with the guard cells, but are formed by cells lying around the meristemoid that divides to form the guard cells;

Mesoperigenous: at least one of the subsidiary cells has a common origin with the guard cells, but the others do not.

The mesogenous type of stoma thus corresponds to the syndetocheilic, and the perigenous to the haplocheilic, type of stomata described by Florin[109] for gymnosperms, but these terms are not now used exclusively in an ontogenetic sense. Obviously, it would not be possible to classify

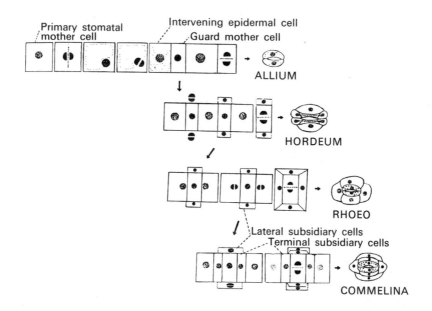

Fig. 7.12 Types of stomata of monocotyledonous plants. The method of formation of guard cells and subsidiary cells, and the ultimate spatial relationships between them, are shown in *Allium, Hordeum, Rhoeo* and *Commelina.* (From Stebbins and Jain,[244] Fig. 1, p. 413.)

stomata according to this scheme by observation of adult material only, such as might be found in most herbaria.

These classifications apply to stomata of dicotyledonous plants. Recently four categories of stomatal complex have been recognized in monocotyledons. Two of these categories have four or more subsidiary cells, one has two subsidiaries, and the fourth type has no subsidiary cells differing from the other epidermal cells (Fig. 7.12). Some correlation was found between the type of stomatal complex and various other features, including the type of germination, the growth habit of the mature plant and its geographical distribution. The type with many subsidiary cells was considered to be the most primitive.[245]

8

Xylem

The vascular system of the plant is made up of xylem, the water-conducting tissue, and phloem, the food-conducting tissue. Since an adequate supply of water and food is obviously essential for growth, it is at once evident that the vascular system is functionally very important within the plant. The possession of vascular tissues separates the higher plants from some of the more primitive groups of plants which are devoid of comparable conducting tissues. Many of the components of the xylem are hard and thick-walled, and are thus usually better preserved in fossil materials than the soft-walled phloem. Consequently, the phylogeny of xylem is better understood than that of the phloem. For other reasons also, the xylem is easier to study than the phloem, and will be considered first.

Hardwood and softwood timbers, many of which are of great commercial value, are made up of the secondary xylem of dicotyledons and gymnosperms respectively (see Part 2, Chapter 4). Wood is not only used for various constructional purposes, but is also the raw material of paper. In the U.S.A. alone, 25 million tons of paper and paperboard are made each year.[22] Consequently xylem is of considerable economic importance, as well as being of great functional importance to the plant.

Origin

During the primary growth of the plant, xylem differentiates from the procambium, situated below the growing root or shoot apex or associated with a leaf primordium. The procambium consists of meristematic, densely cytoplasmic cells elongated in the longitudinal plane of the organ in which it occurs. The differentiation of primary xylem and phloem from this tissue is described in Part 2, Chapters 2 and 3. The first elements of the primary xylem to differentiate and become mature are known as the *protoxylem*; those which mature later are called *metaxylem*. In plants which undergo secondary growth, i.e. most gymnosperms and dicotyledons, the vascular cambium gives rise to secondary xylem. The patterns in which the elements of the xylem and phloem differentiate differ in the various organs of the plant. Differentiation of vascular tissues in these organs, and the controlling factors involved, are considered in Part 2.

Elements of the xylem

Xylem is a complex tissue, composed of the conducting or tracheary elements, fibres and parenchyma. Xylary fibres are elongated elements with pointed ends and are thought to have evolved from tracheids. They usually have thicker walls and the pits may have smaller borders than the tracheids of the same species.[91] Recent evidence[106,107] suggests that wood fibres may retain living protoplasts for as long as twenty years, although they are usually defined as non-living elements. Further studies of xylary fibres from a considerable number of species seem advisable. There may be transitional types between fibres and tracheids. Living parenchyma cells are present in both primary and secondary xylem. They may contain starch or crystals, and fulfil a storage function; eventually they too may become lignified.

Tracheary elements are of two kinds, tracheids and vessel members. Both types are of elongated cells, thick-walled and usually devoid of living contents at maturity. The cell contents may be discernible up to the time of lignification of the wall. The secondary wall thickening is laid down in various patterns and usually becomes lignified. *Tracheids* originate from single cells, are normally elongated and pointed at both ends, and are imperforate, i.e. the primary wall is always continuous, pit-closing membranes being present in the regions of pits. Tracheids are present in all groups of vascular plants, and the tracheary elements of most pteridophytes and gymnosperms consist exclusively of tracheids (Fig. 8.1).

By contrast, *vessel members* are perforate elements aggregated longitudinally into files of cells connected through the pores or perforations. These chains of cells are vessels, and may vary from two cells to an indefinite but considerable length, perhaps several feet. More information on vessel length is required. Vessels of the primary and secondary xylem are thus formed from a longitudinal file of procambial or cambial cells respectively. Vessels are present in the wood of nearly all angiosperms; the exceptions are certain members of the Ranales, an order of plants usually considered to be relatively primitive, which have very uniform

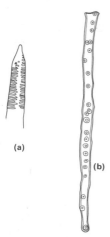

(a)

(b)

Fig. 8.1   Tracheids. (**a**) Part of a tracheid of *Polypodium*, showing scalariform pitting.   × 180. (**b**) Tracheid of *Pinus*, showing circular bordered pits.   × 115.

wood composed almost entirely of tracheids. Vessels are absent from the wood of most gymnosperms and pteridophytes.

Xylem elements which differentiate during early phases of growth, i.e. protoxylem elements, usually have a thin primary wall with rings or helices of secondary wall thickening deposited upon it. These annular or helical (spiral) xylem elements (Fig. 8.2a, b) are extensible and often become much stretched during the elongation of the organ in which they occur. During this process the original rings or helices of secondary wall material become more widely separated. The later-formed elements of the

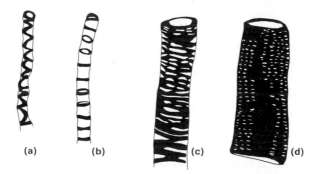

(a)   (b)   (c)   (d)

Fig. 8.2   Vessel members from the primary xylem of *Phaseolus* showing different types of secondary wall thickening. (**a**) Spiral or helical; (**b**) annular; (**c**) partially pitted and partially reticulate; (**d**) pitted. Secondary wall shown black. Only parts of a vessel member are shown in (**a**)–(**c**). (**a**)–(**d**) × 240.

metaxylem or of the secondary xylem have much more extensive regions of secondary wall; these are reticulate or pitted elements (Fig. 8.2c, d). A recent comparative study of the primary xylem from some 1,350 species of angiosperms indicates that these later-maturing elements are in fact ontogenetically derived from the helical elements by the deposition of additional secondary wall material between the gyres of the existing helix. Bierhorst and Zamora[26] interpret the secondary wall system of tracheary elements as consisting of a first-order framework (the helical system) and a second-order framework (additional secondary wall deposited between the gyres of the helix). The fact that elements in intermediate stages of development are observed only relatively infrequently is attributed by these authors to the occurrence of such elements in only some vascular bundles of certain internodes of the stem. Occasionally, however, all stages of development of the secondary wall may be observed in a single rapidly-elongating element. In terms of this view of the development of tracheary

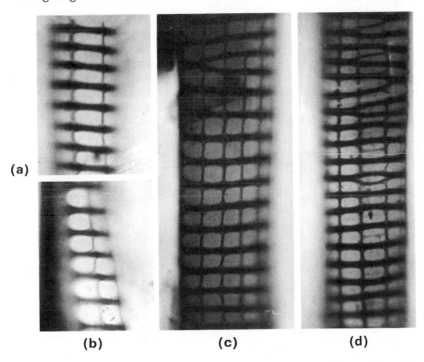

(a)

(b)   (c)   (d)

Fig. 8.3 Portions of the metaxylem of *Aneilema vitiense* (Commelinaceae), showing presence of a primary framework of wall thickenings and progressive formation of the secondary framework. × 650. (From Bierhorst and Zamora,[26] Figs. 128–131, p. 669.)

elements, annular and helical components could be considered to be juvenile forms showing a type of arrested development. It is interesting to consider why the second-order framework should be deposited only on the later-maturing elements. It is known that exposure to light accelerates secondary wall deposition,[122,239] but the mechanism involved is not fully understood.

In a number of genera of the family Commelinaceae the development of the second-order framework can be seen particularly clearly.[26] The metaxylem elements may be helical or annular, and these thickenings of the primary framework become interconnected by a very uniform system of vertical strands, the developing second-order framework (Fig. 8.3). These vertical strands are themselves occasionally interconnected by transverse strands or sheets of second-order framework (Fig. 8.3d).

Perforation plates

The region of the wall of a vessel member in which a pore or perforation occurs is known as the perforation plate. These plates are usually terminal in position, but may be sub-terminal or lateral; the perforation may be *simple*, with one pore (Fig. 8.4c) or multiple, with more than one. In multiple perforation plates, the pores may be arranged in various ways. When the pores occur in a ladder-like arrangement, with intervening bars of thickening, the perforation plate is *scalariform*, e.g. *Liriodendron*, the tulip tree (Fig. 8.4a). When the perforations are more or less circular and

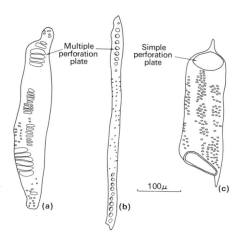

Fig. 8.4 Perforation plates in vessel members. (a) Scalariform (*Liriodendron*); (b) foraminate (*Ephedra*); (c) simple (*Quercus*) perforation plates. Pits are also shown. × 115.

are grouped together, the perforation plate is *foraminate*, e.g. *Ephedra*, one of the few gymnosperms that possesses vessels (Fig. 8.4b). If numerous small pores are separated by a network of secondary wall thickening, these form a *reticulate* perforation plate. Simple perforation plates are thought to have been phylogenetically derived from the multiple type, by loss of the bars of thickening. At least in later-formed xylem elements, a slight thickening may be present on the region of the primary wall that later becomes the perforation; subsequently it disappears gradually.[26,85]

Fine structure of xylem elements

In an electron microscopic study of parenchyma cells of *Coleus* which had been induced to differentiate into thickened xylem cells as a result of wounding (see below), Hepler and Newcomb[134] reported a concentration of organelles and vesicles along the cytoplasmic bands occupying the sites of subsequent wall thickenings. Dense strands of cytoplasm which foreshadowed the positions of the secondary wall had been reported much earlier from studies with the light microscope.[69,227] In studies of the differentiation of the normal xylem of *Acer*, *Beta*, *Cucurbita*, and of the *Avena* coleoptile, however, no indication of any regular distribution of cytoplasm and organelles in relation to wall thickenings was observed with the electron microscope.[67,98,285] However, microtubules have been observed in close association with the developing secondary wall thickenings, both in normally differentiating tracheary elements of *Acer*,[285] *Avena*[67] and *Cucurbita*[99] and in xylem cells induced to regenerate from parenchyma in *Coleus*[135] and *Nicotiana*.[66] In young tracheary elements, dense cytoplasm is present, and dictyosomes and rough endoplasmic reticulum are especially prominent. In the later stages of differentiation, after the deposition of wall thickenings, both the endoplasmic reticulum and various organelles break down.[101,285] These degenerative changes are comparable with those that occur in differentiating sieve elements (see Chapter 9).

Phylogeny

A considerable amount of work has been done on the phylogenetic trends shown by the xylem elements, since these elements are relatively conservative and also often remain well preserved in fossil materials.

Vessel elements are considered to have evolved from tracheids, and to have developed independently and in a parallel fashion in the various groups in which they occur.[20,50] In the dicotyledons vessels appeared first in the secondary xylem, and only subsequently in the primary xylem; in monocotyledons, which usually have no secondary xylem, vessels occurred first in the oldest parts of the primary xylem. It is believed that they occurred first in the roots, and only later in the stems and aerial parts of the plant.[51,53] In this connection, the recent report[279] that in ferns the most highly evolved tracheids (and, in species in which they occur, vessels) occur in the roots rather than the aerial parts is of considerable interest.

In general, the specialization of vessel elements has gone from long narrow elements with tapering ends, to short, wide, squat elements with approximately transverse end walls. Scalariform perforation plates are considered to be the most primitive type and simple perforations the most highly evolved.[50] A statistical correlation has been shown between long vessel elements, very oblique end walls, and perforation plates with many bars.[48] All of these are considered to be primitive or unspecialized characters. The arrangement of pits is also usually considered to have progressed from scalariform through opposite to alternate, but Bierhorst and Zamora[26] have recently pointed out that only slight modifications during ontogeny are required to transform opposite into alternate pits. From their observations on the xylem of a large number of living species, these authors also drew the general conclusion that there is a general trend of specialization in the xylem which expresses itself in the ever earlier appearance during ontogeny of advanced features and the elimination of primitive ones.

CONTROL OF DIFFERENTIATION OF XYLEM ELEMENTS

One of the most interesting problems of differentiation is the development of procambial or cambial cells into both xylem and phloem. These are tissues with distinctive physiological and anatomical characteristics and very different functions in the plant; yet they differentiate from the same precursors and in close spatial relationship. A considerable body of interesting experimental work is accumulating which throws some light on the factors controlling xylem differentiation, but much still remains to be done.

Genetic aspects

Differentiation of xylem, as of other tissues, is clearly under overall genetic control, and some interesting mutants exist which have been investigated from an anatomical standpoint. For example, a recessive mutant of maize, designated *wilted*, shows severe signs of wilting during most of the growing period, even when the soil is kept well moistened. Anatomical studies showed that the wilting was attributable to the greatly retarded differentiation of the two large metaxylem elements in the vascular bundles of the stem (compare Fig. 8.5b and c with 8.5a).[203] During later stages of development most of the vessel elements did differentiate, and the wilting symptoms were alleviated. In another single-gene mutant, *wilty-*

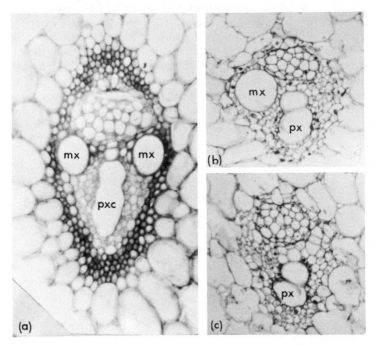

Fig. 8.5 Vascular bundles from transverse sections of stems of *Zea mays*. (a) From a normal plant. (b) and (c) From *wilted*, a recessive mutant. In (b) one large metaxylem element (mx) is present, but only slightly differentiated. In (c) no large metaxylem elements have differentiated. px, protoxylem; pxc, protoxylem canal. × 200. (Material of *wilted* by courtesy of Dr. S. N. Postlethwait.)

dwarf tomato, the water deficit leading to wilting symptoms was again attributable to anomalous vessel development. In this instance, secondary wall material was deposited across the primary end wall prior to its breakdown to form the perforation plate. This was considered to be due to the failure of a control mechanism during development.[3]

These examples illustrate the effects of single gene change on the differentiation of a xylem element once this has been initiated. What controls the initial differentiation of a cell as a tracheary element? The results of many experiments indicate that auxin is closely implicated.

Effects of auxin

Some sixty years ago, Simon[223] found that if incisions were made in the vascular strands of a stem, so that these were interrupted, new xylem cells differentiated from the parenchymatous cells of the pith, and these formed between two vascular bundles. This work was later extended by Sinnott and Bloch,[226,227] who used plants of *Coleus*, which has pairs of opposite leaves. They showed that vascular strands did not always regenerate between the apical and basal ends of a single severed vascular bundle, but sometimes did so also between this bundle and another across the stem from it. In the pith cells in the path of this future vascular strand divisions took place and oblique walls were formed, apparently along a new axis of polarity (Fig. 8.6a). Later bands of lignin were laid down on the

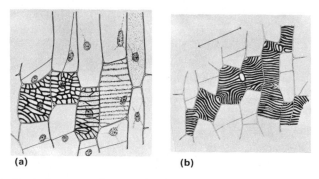

(a)   (b)

Fig. 8.6 Parts of regenerating strands of xylem elements in the pith of wounded stems of *Coleus*. (a) Recent cell divisions in the pith cells are evident, and stages in the differentiation and lignification of the ringed and reticulate patterns in the cell walls. On the right, bands of cytoplasm indicate the places where lignified thickenings will later differentiate.   × 212. (b) Pattern of lignified bands in the cell walls and the position of pores, 8 days after wounding. The new cell walls and the line of pores are parallel to the course of the new strand (arrow). × 150. (From Sinnott and Bloch,[227] Figs. 7 and 9, pp. 152 and 154.)

walls of these parenchymatous cells. Pores were present in some of the cells (Fig. 8.6b). Sinnott and Bloch[227] noted that the first sign of the lignified thickenings was a reorientation of the cytoplasm into granular bands around the cell, occupying the position of the future bands of lignin. Twenty years later Hepler and Newcomb,[134] working with the electron microscope, reported the aggregation of cell organelles in these positions in regenerating xylem cells; however, as already mentioned, such aggregations have not been observed in normal xylem.[67,285] Sinnott and Bloch[226] also pointed out that the pattern of wall thickening was often continuous from one cell to another, and drew the conclusion that the cytoplasmic changes occurring in a cell during its differentiation do not take place in isolation but are an integral part of the changes taking place in a group of related cells.

It seems likely that some sort of gradient is established along the new axis of polarity of the regenerating strand. After considering all the information available at the time, Jacobs[140-142] designed a series of experiments to investigate the view that an auxin gradient might be involved and, further, that auxin was a limiting factor in xylem regeneration (see Appendix). Jacobs wounded internodes of *Coleus*, and observed the regeneration of xylem under various conditions. In some experiments leaves and buds distal or proximal to the wound were removed. He established that neither auxin transport nor xylem regeneration in the stem was wholly basipetal (i.e. from apex to base), as had been believed, but that there was a quantitative relationship between the amount of acropetal or basipetal auxin transport and the amount of acropetal or basipetal xylem regeneration (Fig. 8.7). Jacobs[140] also showed that a young leaf distal to the wound

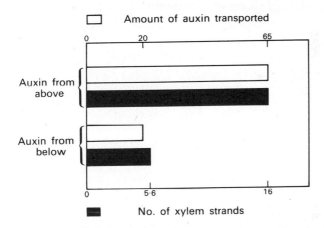

Fig. 8.7 Histogram showing the relationship between the amount of auxin transported in isolated sections of the stem of *Coleus* and the number of strands of xylem regenerated when the leaves above and below are excised. (From Jacobs,[142] Fig. 2, p. 165. By permission of the University of Chicago Press.)

had a stimulatory effect on xylem regeneration, and that this effect could be simulated by applying indoleacetic acid (IAA) to the cut stump of the petiole of an excised leaf or to a decapitated internode (Fig. 8.8). These findings indicated that auxin was a limiting factor in the regeneration of xylem under these experimental conditions. The capacity of the internode for transporting auxin is also implicated. This view is supported by experiments in which the amount of regeneration was reduced when tri-iodobenzoic acid (a substance which blocks auxin transport) was applied

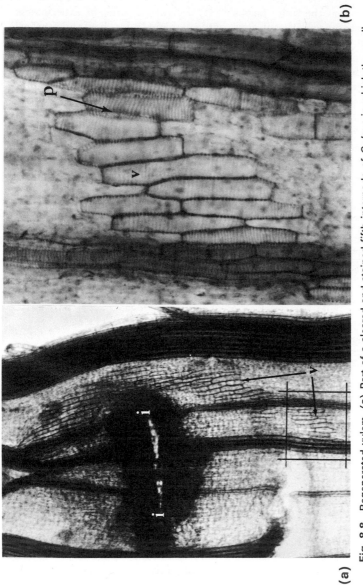

Fig. 8.8 Regenerated xylem. **(a)** Part of a cleared and stained fifth internode of *Coleus* in which the small central vascular bundle has been incised (i–i, incision.) The stem was excised above the fifth node and all leaves and buds were removed; 1% indoleacetic acid in lanolin was applied to the cut surface. Wound vessel members (v) have regenerated around the wound, from parenchymatous cells. One week after treatment. *See* Appendix. ×30. **(b)** Part of a enclosed in rectangle, enlarged. p, pore. ×150.

between the wound and the applied IAA.[257] By a careful study of normal differentiation in the shoot of *Coleus* it was later shown[143] that auxin was a limiting factor in the differentiation of normal xylem also. There is a precise quantitative relationship between the rate of production of diffusible auxin and of xylem cells in a particular internode in the normal development (Fig. 8.9). The amount of auxin required to induce the differentiation of a parenchyma cell as a regenerated tracheary cell is approximately 14 times that required for normal differentiation from a procambial cell.[143]

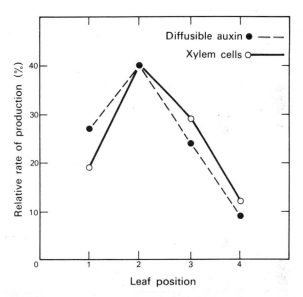

Fig. 8.9 Relative rates of production of diffusible auxin and xylem elements in normally differentiating unwounded plants of *Coleus* in relation to leaf position on the plant (the production of leaves 1–4 inclusive is taken as 100%). (From Jacobs and Morrow,[143] Fig. 16, p. 838.)

In further work on xylem regeneration in *Coleus*, it has been shown[206] that severance of the primary xylem only does not result in the regeneration of xylem elements from pith cells, but it is not certain whether the factors involved resulted from the severance of the primary phloem only or from that of both the phloem and xylem. An interesting effect of auxin concentration was demonstrated in experiments in which 2 mm stem segments of *Coleus* were grown in aseptic culture.[114] Xylem elements differentiated in the slices even on the control medium; addition of indoleacetic acid (IAA), 2,4-dichlorophenoxyacetic acid (2,4-D), tri-iodobenzoic acid or kinetin inhibited differentiation of these elements, but low concentrations of IAA or 2,4-D led to over 100% increase in the number formed. It is possible that high concentrations of these substances may inhibit the polar transport of auxin.

The importance of auxin in controlling the differentiation of tracheary elements is further indicated by experiments in which pith excised from herbaceous stems was grown in aseptic culture, and sterile micro-pipettes containing aqueous solutions of IAA, kinetin or both these substances were inserted into the pith. In tobacco pith small areas of dividing cells developed just below the tip of the pipette, and xylem tracheids occurred among them in a haphazard manner. No cell divisions were associated with empty pipettes or those containing only sterile water.[55] In cabbage pith various results were obtained, including the differentiation of xylem elements, depending on the ratio of kinetin to IAA.[56]

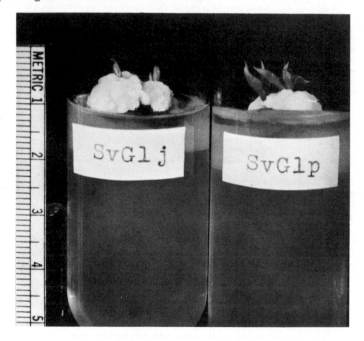

Fig. 8.10 Shoot apices of *Syringa vulgaris* grafted into callus of the same species, after 7 weeks in culture. (From Wetmore and Sorokin,[273] Pl. 1, Fig. 1.)

Experiments with callus

In addition to pith, undifferentiated callus tissue has been used for studies of vascular differentiation. Callus is unorganized tissue in which parenchymatous cells are randomly arranged and usually no other cell types are present. When a growing shoot apex of lilac (*Syringa vulgaris*) was grafted into callus of the same species and maintained in aseptic culture on a defined medium, vascular tissue differentiated in the callus (Figs. 8.10, 8.11).[47,273] Substitution of the scion by a block of agar containing physiological concentrations of auxin gave similar results; nodules of vascular tissue were formed in the callus at some distance from the graft, the distance depending on the concentration of auxin. This work was

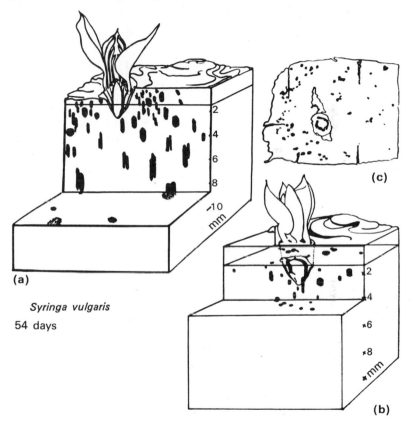

Fig. 8.11 (a) and (b) Three-dimensional diagrams of a piece of lilac callus (*Syringa vulgaris*) into which an apex of the same species with 2 or 3 pairs of leaf primordia was grafted. 1% agar containing 0·05 mg/l. naphthaleneacetic acid was placed in the incision. This is a composite drawing constructed from serial sections taken 54 days after the beginning of the experiment. (c) Transverse section at about the 2 mm mark. Vascular tissue black. (From Wetmore and Sorokin,[273] Figs. 1 and 2, p. 309.)

subsequently extended to five additional species; sucrose and/or IAA were supplied in the agar placed in the cut.[272] When sugar and auxin were placed in the cut on top of the callus and neither was present in the medium, nodules of vascular tissue were formed in a circle below the site of application. When auxin and sugar were present in the culture medium as well, another set of nodules was present towards the base of the callus, below the level of the medium (Fig. 8.12). Both xylem and phloem were present

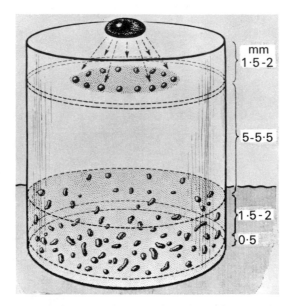

Fig. 8.12 Three-dimensional diagram of a piece of callus of lilac (*Syringa vulgaris*). 1% agar containing 0·1 mg/l. naphthaleneacetic acid and 3% sucrose (or different concentrations of these substances) was applied to the top of the callus, which was grown on a culture medium which also contained these substances. A circle of nodules of vascular tissue (tracheids surrounded by sieve elements) differentiated below the agar block. The diameter of the circle depends on the concentration of auxin. Additional nodules (with phloem towards and xylem away from the medium) were formed below the medium, usually in greatest abundance 1–2 mm from the callus surface. (From Wetmore and Rier,[272] Fig. 12, p. 426.)

in the nodules. Low concentrations (1·5–2·5%) of sugar were found to favour xylem formation, high concentrations (3–4%) phloem; and at intermediate concentrations (2·5–3·5%) both xylem and phloem were formed, usually with cambium in between. Individual nodules showed the normal orientation of vascular tissues found in a stem, i.e. phloem towards the periphery and xylem towards the centre of the callus. Wetmore and

Rier[272] further showed that when sucrose and auxin were supplied through a micro-pipette in the callus, as in the experiments with pith already described, a complete ring of xylem, or of xylem with phloem, differentiated around the pipette. In some experiments cambium was present between the xylem and the phloem.

These experiments thus come close to inducing, in unorganized callus tissue, not only the kinds of tissues, but the arrangements of tissues, normally found in stems (see Part 2, Chapter 3). In the normal development the shoot apex (probably including the young leaf primordia; see Esau[92]) would no doubt be the source of the auxin and sugar required for the differentiation of the vascular tissues. Because of the continuous vertical growth of the shoot tip away from proximal regions of the stem, strands of vascular tissue, instead of nodules at a certain fixed distance from a static source, could result. It is interesting that the induction of vascular tissues seems to have no relation to their ultimate functions in the plant. These experiments have shown, in addition, that not only procambial cells, but any cell supplied with the necessary substances in appropriate concentration, can give rise to xylem or phloem.[272] This contention is supported by the successful induction, with sucrose and an auxin, of tracheids in fern gametophytes which never normally contain such cells.[75]

To the procambium, however, is attributed the important function of giving pattern to the vascular system; the characteristic pattern is blocked out during the procambial phase of development.[271] This pattern is not only under genetic control, but differs fundamentally in the root and the shoot of the same plant (see Part 2, Chapters 2 and 3, where some of the factors involved are discussed).

Thus in recent years knowledge of the factors controlling the differentiation of xylem has been greatly advanced. Further work on xylem is still required, however, not only in this field but in that of phylogeny, comparative anatomy, and others.

9

Phloem

The function of the phloem as the food-conducting tissue of the plant, and the still controversial nature of the mechanism by which this function is fulfilled, have resulted in intensive studies of the anatomy and physiology of this tissue. In particular, the fine structure of phloem elements has recently received much attention. As yet relatively few species have been examined with the electron microscope, however, and therefore the facts described may not prove to be applicable to all plants. Because of the peculiar nature of the phloem elements, they are technically difficult to study; and although much is now known of their structure and ultrastructure many aspects are still incompletely understood, particularly those relating to function.

Origin

As in the case of xylem, the primary phloem differentiates from procambium, and the secondary phloem from the vascular cambium, during primary and secondary growth of the plant respectively. The first elements of the primary phloem to mature are known as protophloem; subsequently differentiating components constitute the metaphloem.

As already indicated, the differentiation of two tissues—phloem and xylem—so dissimilar in structure, physiology and function, from the same precursors, and in close spatial proximity, poses a number of developmental problems which have yet to be solved.

Elements of the phloem

Like the xylem, phloem is a complex tissue, composed of several different types of elements. These comprise sieve elements or sieve cells, companion cells, parenchyma, fibres and sclereids. Secretory cells or tissues of various kinds may also be associated with the phloem, e.g. the laticifers in *Hevea*, from which rubber is derived, and oil cells in the secondary phloem of *Cinnamomum*, the source of cinnamon. It has been aptly remarked that the xylem elements themselves are of economic importance, since they constitute the bulk of the wood, whereas in the main the phloem elements are less important economically than are the other tissues associated with them. However, many phloem fibres (e.g. flax) are of considerable commercial value.

Fibres may be present in both primary and secondary phloem. They have thick secondary walls with simple or slightly bordered pits; the walls are often lignified. Phloem fibres are elongated elements with overlapping ends. Protophloem elements often differentiate into fibres in later stages of development. Recent observations[182] of rotation of cytoplasm in phloem fibres suggest that they may conceivably play a role in transport of materials, in addition to providing support. Phloem fibres may be septate in certain plants, e.g. *Vitis* (Fig. 6.7a). Sclereids also often occur in association with the phloem, e.g. in many barks (*Quercus*, oak; *Rhamnus*, cascara; *Cinnamomum*, cinnamon).

Parenchyma cells are present in both primary and secondary phloem. These cells have primary walls with primary pit fields, and living contents; in inactive phloem the cell walls may later become thickened and lignified. The parenchyma cells store starch, resins, etc., and crystals are often present; crystal-containing parenchyma cells may form a sheath around fibres or bundles of fibres, especially in the secondary phloem.

Parenchyma cells may be physiologically related in some way to the sieve elements, like the companion cells, but less closely. Sometimes parenchyma cells die at the same time as a neighbouring sieve element.

Sieve elements

Like the tracheary elements of the xylem, these are of two kinds. *Sieve cells* occur in pteridophytes and gymnosperms; they are single, somewhat elongate cells with specialized sieve areas in their lateral and sometimes also in their terminal walls. *Sieve tubes*, which occur in angiosperms, are longitudinal files of cells, each of which is a sieve tube member. In such cells, one or more of the sieve areas, usually in or near an end wall, is more specialized, and forms a sieve plate. This is a region of the wall comprising a number of pores, through which strands connect one member with another, usually vertically; these are called connecting strands.

Sieve elements are very remarkable cells, indeed unique, for they are living cells which at maturity contain no nucleus. The sieve element has been aptly termed a nonconformist cell.[88] A necrotic nucleus has been observed in the mature sieve cells of *Pinus*,[190] but further observations are undoubtedly required. In most angiosperms, sieve elements are closely associated with living, nucleate cells, the *companion cells*; these originate from the same mother cell as the sieve element, and are thought to have a very close physiological and functional relationship with it throughout life. A careful study of secondary phloem in members of the Calycanthaceae revealed that most sieve elements had one or two, and occasionally up to five, companion cells associated with them ontogenetically; nearly 5%, however, had no associated companion cells.[52] Much information has recently stemmed from studies of phloem elements with the electron microscope, but despite this careful analytical work the development and mode of functioning of the sieve element and its attendant companion cell(s) remain rather enigmatic. Zimmermann[291] has pointed out that the occasional absence of associated companion cells should be taken into account in any consideration of their functional role. Recent suggestions that protoplasmic streaming from one cell to another along transcellular strands[255] is the principal method of translocation have met with opposition, and the most generally supported hypothesis relating to transport in the phloem is probably still one involving mass flow.

In early stages of differentiation, the sieve element is not distinguishable from the neighbouring companion cell, except in size. The sieve element and companion cell are formed by an unequal division of the type already discussed in previous chapters (Fig. 9.1).[41] At an early stage of development, both cells have nuclei and dense cytoplasm, containing mitochondria, dictyosomes, endoplasmic reticulum and in some plants, though not in *Cucurbita*—on which many ultrastructural studies have been carried out— plastids. Discrete *slime bodies* are present in the cells; slime is a proteinaceous substance characteristically found in sieve elements (Fig. 9.2a). One suggestion is that slime is synthesized by the endoplasmic reticulum.[37] Recent observations[68] indicate that in young sieve elements protein appears in the form of compact structures, the slime bodies, these bodies consisting of aggregations of tubules, designated P_1-protein. During the differentiation of the sieve element, the tubules become dispersed in the cytoplasm (Fig. 9.3), and groups of striated fibrils, designated P_2-protein, become evident. It is believed that the P_1-protein gives rise to the P_2-protein. In *Cucurbita*, RNA has been found in slime bodies.[46] As in other plant cells, the vacuole is delimited by a membrane, the tonoplast. In the sieve elements of *Pisum*, at least, numerous microtubules are present in early stages of development, in association with the plasma membrane.[37] During differentiation of the sieve element the mitochondria undergo degenerative changes, and show disorganization of the inner membrane; thus eventually they have few or no cristae.[96] If present, chloroplasts also either fail to develop much internal structure or lose what they have.[37] It has been suggested[230] that

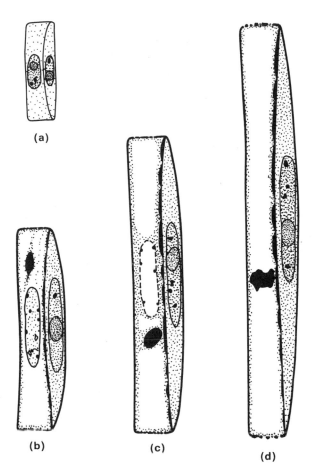

(a)

(b)   (c)

(d)

Fig. 9.1 Semi-diagrammatic views of the development of a sieve tube element and its companion cell. (**a**) Distinction between sieve element (left) and companion cell is mainly one of size. (**b**) The cytoplasm of the two cells is now clearly different. Vacuolation is occurring in the sieve element, and its nucleus is beginning to disappear, whereas that of the companion cell is growing. Pits are present in the cell walls and the formation of slime bodies (black) has begun. (**c**) The nucleus of the sieve element has almost disappeared, and the sieve plate is partially perforated. (**d**) Final stage in differentiation and elongation. The nucleus of the sieve element is lost, and there is only a thin layer of cytoplasm. Pores in the sieve plate are now broken through. Slime bodies are large and lobed. (From Bünning,[41] Fig. 69, p. 74, after Resch.)

the high levels of carbohydrates in sieve elements may be antagonistic to the formation of grana in plastids. The slime bodies become much less

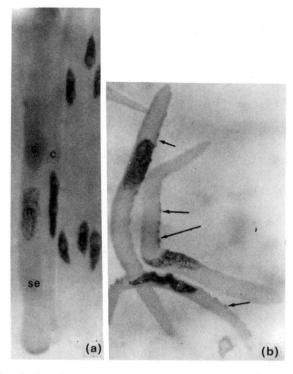

Fig. 9.2   Developing sieve tube elements and companion cells in squash prepara-
tions from young stems of *Vicia faba*. (a) The nucleus (n) of the sieve tube
element (se) is beginning to disintegrate; slime (s) is present. c, companion cell.
×400. (b) Nuclei are becoming lobed. Note the nacreous cell wall (arrowed).
×300.

clearly defined, and eventually fuse together, forming a mass of slime. At
about the same time, according to some observers, the tonoplast breaks
down, so that the vacuolar material mingles with the cytoplasm, forming a
substance which has been termed mictoplasm.[82] Other workers[230] have
failed to observe rupture of the tonoplast and believe that whole vacuoles
are resorbed, so that the concept of mictoplasm would be inappropriate.
Numerous ribosomes are present at this stage.[155] At this time, too, the
endoplasmic reticulum becomes replaced by vesicles and the nucleus
disintegrates.[97] The nucleus ceases to have its former staining properties,
becomes markedly lobed, and the nuclear envelope breaks down. The
nucleoli are set free into the cytoplasm, at least in some species, and later
disappear.[82] The occurrence of this phenomenon in species from closely
related families may be of some phylogenetic significance.[290] At the margin

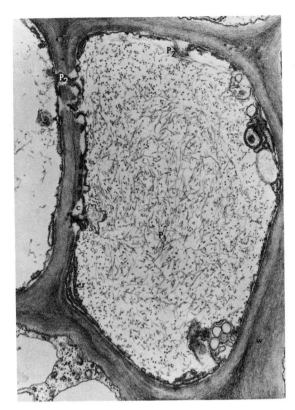

Fig. 9.3 Transverse section of a sieve element of *Nicotiana tabacum* at a late stage of differentiation. P–protein is present in the cell lumen. Both P_1 and P_2 protein are present but the former predominates. c, callose; er, endoplasmic reticulum; w, cell wall. × 15,500. (From Cronshaw and Esau,[68] Fig. 11, p. 813.)

of the sieve tube element is a layer of contents with membranes apparently derived from the endoplasmic reticulum and the nuclear membrane, usually oriented longitudinally.[37]

Delimitation of the sieve plate begins at an early stage of differentiation of the sieve element. Kollmann,[155] working with the gymnosperm *Metasequoia*, found that cell connections through the sieve areas were established early and made the interesting suggestion that the changes in the cell organelles which lead to degeneration of the sieve cells might be considered to be a consequence of, rather than a prerequisite for, the physiological functions of the conducting elements of the phloem. However this may be, it is clear that although recent work on ultrastructure now provides a fairly complete picture of the morphological changes occurring in differentiating sieve elements, the underlying causes of these have as yet scarcely been considered, far less understood.

Sieve elements sometimes have quite thick walls, and such walls have been termed nacreous, because of their glistening properties (Fig. 9.2b). The nacreous cell wall may develop very early in the ontogeny of the sieve element, while it still possesses a nucleus.[27] Formation of the nacreous wall is followed by the disappearance of microtubules.[37] Sometimes the nacreous part of the wall may be distinguishable morphologically from that part of the wall formed still earlier. On occasion it may be very thick, up to half of the diameter of the cell, but it is absent from the region of the sieve plate.[93]

Callose

Callose is a carbohydrate which is formed not only in sieve elements but also in some other types of cells. Apparently enzymes located in the plasmalemma are involved both in the synthesis and breakdown of callose in the sieve element;[65] since the timing of callose synthesis may be critical these enzymes assume some importance in the physiology of phloem.

Callose is found in sieve elements in association with the sieve plate and lateral sieve areas; it forms a sheath around the connecting strands which penetrate the pores in the sieve plate, and in the lateral sieve areas. It is indisputably formed in response to wounding, but much discussion is centred on whether callose is also normally present in uninjured sieve elements. This is obviously an important matter, but since killing material for microscopic study involves wounding it is also one which is very difficult to investigate. Recent experiments carried out by Engleman,[81] in which tissue was killed in an uncut condition by various gaseous or temperature treatments, showed that callose was present in sieve elements of intact plants killed within 4 sec after injury. It seems likely, therefore, that it is a normal component of living sieve elements, which is deposited in more massive amounts as a consequence of wounding. The question of the stage in ontogeny of the sieve element at which callose is formed should also be considered.

In *Vitis*,[87] and no doubt also in other plants, there is a seasonal production of callose; in winter months there is an accumulation of dormancy callose, most of which disappears again on resumption of growth.

Sieve plates

A sieve plate is the region of pores between one sieve tube member and another; thus sieve plates may be compared with perforation plates in the xylem. Sieve plates may be simple, consisting of one region of pores, or compound, consisting of several such regions separated by bars of wall thickening (Fig. 9.4).

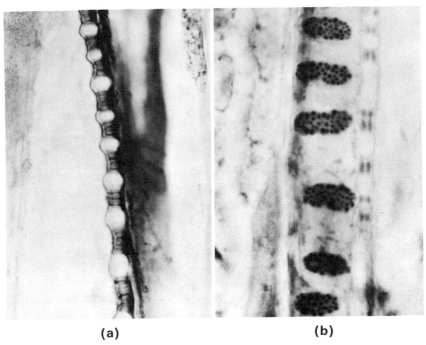

(a)   (b)

Fig. 9.4 Compound sieve plates in *Vitis vinifera*. (a) Sectional view of a sieve plate; darkly stained material is slime. (b) Face view of a sieve plate in a longitudinal wall. The connecting strands surrounded by callose appear as black dots; the whole sieve areas are covered with quantities of callose. × 750. (From Esau,[87] Pl. 12, B and D, p. 288.)

In very early stages of development of the sieve element, when the nucleus is still present, the future sieve plate is smooth and there is no indication of primary pit fields. At a slightly later stage platelets of callose form isolated patches on the cell wall in the sites of the future pores.[37,100] Platelets are paired, occurring on both sides of the cell wall (Fig. 9.5a). At least in some species, endoplasmic reticulum may be discernible applied to localized parts of the wall; the callose appears beneath it. A single plasmodesma is present in each pore site. The platelets of callose increase in thickness, and ultimately the wall material between paired platelets disappears, a break occurs and a pore is formed (Fig. 9.5b). As a consequence of this mode of formation, the pore is lined with callose; this substance thus surrounds the connecting strands (Fig. 9.6). Enzymes are probably involved in the mechanism of perforation;[89] formation of the pores involves more than just the enlargement of existing plasmodesmata, although these may establish the pore sites.[100]

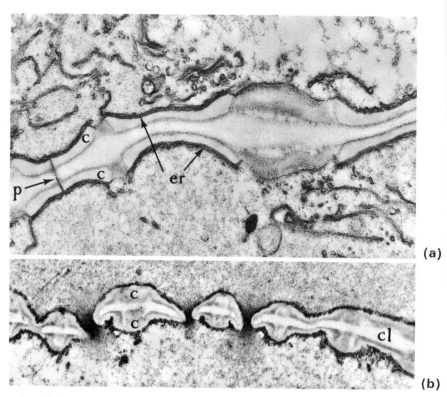

(a)

(b)

Fig. 9.5 Developing sieve plates of *Cucurbita*. (a) Platelets of callose (c) and endoplasmic reticulum (er) are present at the sites of each pore. One pore site is cut through the single plasmodesma (p). × 19,000. (b) Similar view of a sieve plate in which the pores have recently opened. cl, cellulosic part of sieve plate. × 14,000. (From Esau,[89] Figs. 2 and 5, pp. 52 and 54.)

Connecting strands pass through the sieve plate pores from one sieve tube member to another (Fig. 9.7). They may vary in size from the thickness of a plasmodesma to a diameter of about 10 μ. The appearance of connecting strands under the electron microscope is variable; they are usually seen as either solid or composed of fibrillar material.[95,155] It is probable that slime is present in the connecting strands and indeed P_2-protein can be seen in this position (Fig. 9.8).[68] Aggregations of slime known as slime plugs may accumulate at the sieve plate in response to injury to the sieve tube. When the sieve tubes become non-functional the pores of the sieve plate become plugged with callose.

Connection between the sieve elements and companion cells and also

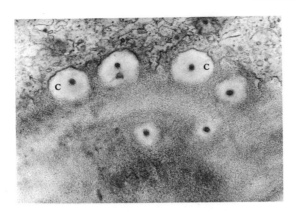

Fig. 9.6 Oblique longitudinal section of a developing sieve plate of *Pisum sativum.* Callose (c) has accumulated round the connecting strands. ×16,000. (From Bouck and Cronshaw,[37] Fig. 10, p. 91.)

parenchyma is maintained by means of plasmodesmata; those situated in the lateral sieve areas are single strands on the side of the sieve element, but branched or multiple on the side of the companion cell.[89,155]

Companion cells

The companion cell is formed from the same mother cell as the sieve tube element adjacent to it (Fig. 9.1), but remains alive and filled with dense protoplasm after the sieve element has ceased to function. Companion cells are of smaller diameter than sieve elements, and are usually somewhat angular in cross section. Observations with the electron microscope show that abundant organelles and membrane systems are present in the cytoplasm of the companion cells; both dictyosomes and endoplasmic reticulum occur and the mitochondria have well marked cristae.[97] Numerous ribosomes have been observed, contributing to the density of the cytoplasm and indicating the occurrence of active protein synthesis.[286] The nucleus, bounded by a normal double membrane, is usually rather elongated and may be lobed. The plastids show little internal structure, but in *Acer*, at least, are closely sheathed with endoplasmic reticulum, connected to the nuclear envelope and the cytoplasmic endoplasmic reticulum. It is suggested that the endoplasmic reticulum linking the plastids and the plasmodesmata may be a route for the transfer of sucrose from the sieve tubes to other neighbouring tissues, the plastids possibly providing temporary storage.[287]

The evidence seems to support the view that the companion cells and other nucleate cells probably form with the sieve elements a complex functional system for the transport of solutes.

5*

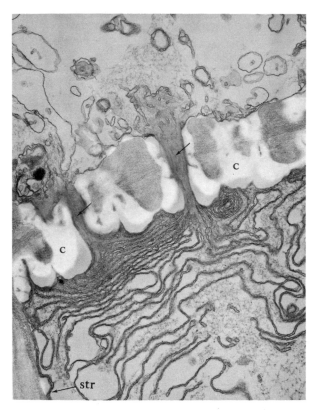

Fig. 9.7 Longitudinal section of mature sieve plate of *Pisum sativum*. The fibrous material filling the pores is arrowed. Many cisternae, which resemble the sieve tube reticulum (str) at the margin of the sieve tube element, are accumulated near the sieve plate. c, callose. × 26,500. (From Bouck and Cronshaw,[37] Fig. 12, p. 95.)

Phylogeny

The evolutionary history of phloem is on the whole less well understood than that of xylem. Sieve elements are thought to have evolved from parenchyma cells, and it is evident that because of the specialized physiology of sieve elements there must have been profound changes in enzyme systems within the cell.[102]

Long sieve tube members with inclined end walls often have compound sieve plates, and these are probably the most primitive type of sieve element. The length of sieve tube members, however, is often deceptive, since trans-

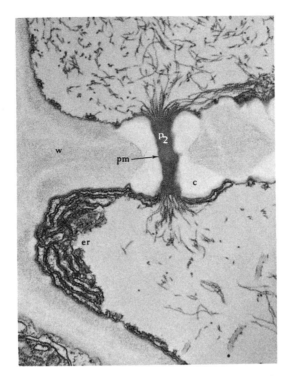

Fig. 9.8 Longitudinal section of sieve element of *Nicotiana tabacum* at a late stage of differentiation. The section passes medianly through a sieve plate pore. The plasma membrane (pm) is continuous through the pore, which is filled with P_2-protein fibrils. The endoplasmic reticulum (er) is closely applied to the plasma membrane of the sieve elements. c, callose; w, wall. ×31,000. (From Cronshaw and Esau,[68] Fig. 10, p. 810.)

verse divisions of cambial derivatives may occur during the formation of the phloem, resulting in shorter elements. More specialized sieve elements are often characterized by relatively transverse end walls and fewer, thick connecting strands.[94,136] There are statistical correlations between long end walls and possession of compound sieve plates, and between approximately horizontal end walls and simple sieve plates.[290]

Cheadle and Whitford[54] found that the least specialized types of phloem elements occurred in the roots of monocotyledons, and more highly specialized types in the aerial parts of the plant, the reverse of the findings relating to xylem elements. Perhaps physiological conditions in the various organs of the plant may be involved, although these observations remain puzzling.

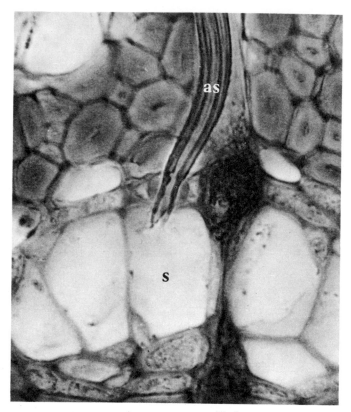

Fig. 9.9 Transverse section of stem of *Tilia* showing the penetration of an aphid stylet (as) into a single sieve tube element (s). The stylet has passed through the phloem fibres.   ×1125. (From Zimmermann,[292] p. 132. Copyright © (1963) by Scientific American, Inc. All rights reserved.)

Viruses in phloem

Some viruses pathogenic to plants are restricted to the phloem tissue. Often these are transported from plant to plant by insect vectors, e.g. aphids, which introduce the virus into part of the phloem, whence it is translocated through the plant. This offers a means of studying rates of transport in the phloem. Thus curly top virus was found to move 15 cm within 6 min in *Beta* (beet), and at least 30 cm in 3 hr in *Cuscuta* (dodder).[88]

Rates of transport can also be calculated from the rate of flow of phloem sap up the severed stylets of aphids. These stylets penetrate the sieve elements very accurately (Fig. 9.9); if the body of the aphid is severed after it has achieved penetration of the sieve tube, leaving the stylet in the

plant tissues, phloem sap continues to be exuded from the stylet for a pro-
longed period. The sap can be collected with a micro-pipette and its compo-
sition studied. The rate of exudation may be more than 5 mm^3 per hr,
which demands refilling of the sieve element 3–10 times per sec and rates of
translocation of the order of 100 cm per hr.[292] It is no wonder that sieve
elements are structurally so specialized.

Insects which feed on phloem often excrete some of the sugar in the form
of a concentrated solution known as honeydew. This honeydew is believed
to have been the manna used by the Israelites in the desert.[88]

CONTROL OF PHLOEM DIFFERENTIATION

In attempts to investigate the factors controlling the differentiation of
phloem a number of experiments have been carried out; most of these
approaches to the problem parallel those employed in the study of xylem.

Using *Coleus* plants, LaMotte and Jacobs[160] studied the regeneration of
phloem in the vicinity of severed vascular bundles under various conditions
(see Appendix). Incisions were made in the flat side of the internode below
the fifth pair of expanded leaves, severing one or more vascular bundles.
Under these conditions, there was regeneration of strands of phloem
elements in the pith; many of these were formed in a plane diagonal to the
long axis of existing cells (Fig. 9.10).[159] In a series of experiments, either
all leaves, all buds, both buds and leaves, buds and leaves distal to the
wound, or buds and leaves proximal to the wound, were removed. A technique for clearing and mounting the injured internode was devised which
made it possible to reach a quantitative estimate of the number of sieve
tube elements regenerated[159] (see Appendix). Removal of all leaves and
buds, and to a lesser extent removal of all organs distal to the wound,
greatly reduced the regeneration of phloem.

In another series of experiments, indoleacetic acid (IAA) in lanolin or in
aqueous solution was applied to the cut stump of wounded stems from
which all organs had been removed; sucrose was also applied.[160] IAA
applied in this way induced more regeneration than the organs of the intact
shoot; sucrose had little effect (Table 9.1). Regeneration of phloem in
excised internodes was also stimulated by IAA, although in this instance
some regeneration took place in controls.

That regenerated sieve elements of this kind are able to function normally is shown clearly by the experiments of Eschrich[103] on wounded stems
of *Impatiens*. He found that a dye could be transported even in the undifferentiated strand of regenerated phloem before the formation of sieve
plates; after this stage the sieve tubes formed as a result of wounding were
fully functional.

LaMotte and Jacobs[160] concluded that auxin normally derived from the

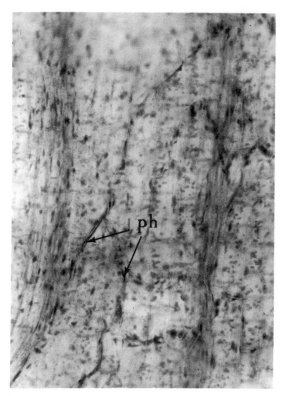

Fig. 9.10 Cleared, stained preparation of a wounded fifth internode of *Coleus* showing regeneration of a strand of phloem (ph) from parenchyma cells between vascular strands. *See* Appendix.   × 150.

lateral organs of the shoot was probably a limiting factor in phloem regeneration. In subsequent experiments with intact plants of *Coleus* it was shown that the regeneration of sieve tubes preceded that of xylem cells by one day.[256] Xylem differentiated adjacent to existing sieve elements. These observations suggest that the primary action of the IAA may be on the regeneration of phloem. The importance attributed[206] to severing the primary phloem may support this view. It is pointed out[256] that this pattern of regeneration—sieve elements, then xylem—resembles that of normal differentiation in a primary stem. In many species the differentiation of secondary phloem also often precedes that of secondary xylem by several weeks.[104]

Table 9.1   The effects of IAA and sucrose on phloem regeneration in plants of *Coleus* without shoot organs. (From LaMotte and Jacobs[160].)

Treatment	Mean number of strands regenerated in 5 days
Controls (intact plants)	$34 \cdot 6 \pm 2 \cdot 8$
All shoot organs off	
Plain lanolin	$9 \cdot 1 \pm 1 \cdot 7$
0·1% IAA in lanolin	$42 \cdot 8 \pm 1 \cdot 4$
1% IAA in lanolin	$64 \cdot 1 \pm 11 \cdot 4$
Water	$13 \cdot 2 \pm 5 \cdot 2$
Water*	$11 \cdot 2 \pm 0 \cdot 9$
20 g/l. sucrose*	$14 \cdot 6 \pm 3 \cdot 7$

* 0.025% sulphanilamide present in the aqueous solution.

There was evidence from some of the experiments discussed above, also, that both sugar and unidentified substances leaking from the cut strands of phloem might sometimes be limiting. Previous observations on normal differentiation in *Coleus* suggested that differentiation of sieve tube elements is normally limited by a factor which moves upwards from the more mature parts of the shoot.[144]

The experiments of Wetmore and Rier[272] on callus, already discussed (see p. 102), indicate that the balance between sucrose and auxin may be critical in controlling the differentiation of cells as xylem or phloem. It is interesting that well developed sieve elements can occur at random in callus cultures, grown on a medium containing an auxin and sucrose but not otherwise treated,[230] in addition to the xylem cells which have been frequently observed. The situation in the wounding experiments with *Coleus* differs from that in undifferentiated callus in that various gradients must already have been set up in the stem; it is noteworthy that xylem regenerates in proximity to the xylem of the severed vascular bundle, and phloem near existing phloem. This is an example of homoeogenetic induction—the induction by a tissue of the differentiation of adjacent tissue in a similar manner. Several earlier experiments also yield evidence of this phenomenon.[40]

From a consideration of these experiments it is clear that several attempts to understand the causes underlying the differentiation of phloem have already been made. However, one needs only to recall the extremely complex changes which occur at the sub-cellular level during the differentiation of sieve elements to conclude that scarcely a beginning has been made in attempting to understand the underlying causes of such changes or the inter-relationships between neighbouring cells in the phloem.

10

Secretory Cells and Tissues

In many species throughout the plant kingdom, cells or whole tissue regions are involved in the processes of secretion or excretion. Secretory cells occur in different parts of the plant and particular kinds of secretory structures are sometimes characteristic of certain families.

Secretion implies the release of substances produced in the cytoplasm and moved outside the cell. These substances may be of no further use to the plant, in which case the process may more properly be defined as excretion, or they may be functionally important, as in the case of hormones or enzymes. However, the borderline between secretion and excretion remains ill-defined, largely because the function of many plant secretions is often still obscure. Many of the products secreted by plants, however, are of considerable economic importance; among these may be mentioned rubber, gutta-percha and opium.

It is difficult to classify structures so diverse as those involved in secretion, since individual structures sometimes transcend particular categories. One simple way to subdivide them is to consider those which secrete substances to the exterior separately from internal secretory tissues.

EXTERNAL SECRETORY STRUCTURES

Some secretory structures, such as the glandular trichomes, are of epidermal origin and are thus completely external. Others comprise both epidermal and more deep-seated tissues.

Glandular trichomes

These plant hairs have already been briefly described in Chapter 7. They have a stalk and a head region; the stalk may be unicellular or multicellular, and may even have several rows of cells. The head, which is the secretory part, may also be unicellular (Fig. 7.8d) or multicellular (Fig. 10.2). The formation of glandular trichomes on the leaves of *Callitriche* is illustrated in Fig. 10.1. The first step is outgrowth of the wall of an epidermal cell, and

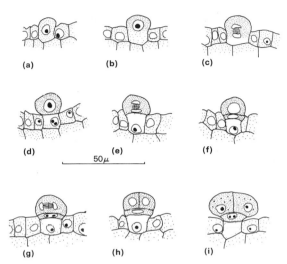

Fig. 10.1 Stages in the development of glandular trichomes on the leaf of *Callitriche*. (a) Elongation of an epidermal cell; cytoplasm uniformly distributed. (b) Cytoplasm now denser towards the outer region of the cell. (c) Telophase in the epidermal cell; cytoplasm unequally distributed. (d) Formation of the glandular, densely cytoplasmic, head cell. (e) Telophase in this cell. (f) Formation of the supporting cell; cytoplasm less dense than that of the head cell, but much denser than that of the mother epidermal cell. (g) Telophase in the head cell (prior divisions may have occurred in other planes). (h) Formation of 2 head cells in this plane. (i) Head region now multicellular. Cytoplasm contains larger particles, perhaps related to the secretory function of the cells. × 430.

unequal distribution of the cytoplasm, which accumulates at the outer end of the cell. Cell division follows, giving a densely cytoplasmic, unicellular head and a vacuolated supporting cell. This is thus another example of the importance of unequal cell divisions in differentiation (see Chapter 2). Further division of the head cell follows, but the cytoplasm remains more or less uniformly distributed. The cells of the head of glandular trichomes are covered with a cuticle, beneath which the secretion accumulates. The cuticle is apparently permeable, but no pores have been observed.[216,219] Trichomes of this type secrete volatile oils, e.g. peppermint oil, balsams, resins and camphors. Some variation in form occurs; for example, in mint the head usually has eight cells and has a rather scale-like appearance in surface view. In the trichomes of *Cannabis* the head is rather similar, but the stalk is multicellular; a type of resin is secreted. The sticky, resinous secretion which is readily seen on the dormant winter buds of many woody plants is a product of glandular trichomes.

Some trichomes of this type may be regarded as nectaries or hydathodes (see below), since they secrete nectar or water respectively. The extra-floral nectaries on the stipules of *Vicia sepium* consist of groups of trichomes.[129] Trichomes functioning as hydathodes occur on the leaves of the aquatic plant *Hygrophila*,[204] as well as in other species.

Numerous specialized trichomes of great interest occur on the leaves of insectivorous plants. Two kinds of glandular hairs, stalked and sessile, are present on the leaves of *Pinguicula*. The stalked glands, which have a 16-celled head, secrete mucilage and are believed to catch small insects; the sessile hairs have only eight cells in the head and secrete an acidic exudate containing a digestive enzyme (Fig. 10.2a, b). The digestive glands of many carnivorous (insectivorous) plants contain a proteolytic enzyme; they are thought to have evolved from hydathodes.[129]

In *Drosophyllum*, both stalked glands that secrete a mucilage which is effective in capturing insects and sessile ones secreting digestive enzymes are again present. The mucilage is secreted by the outer cells of the stalked glands or tentacles, in which many dictyosomes are present; it is believed to be secreted by these organelles.[216,217] Studies of the fine structure of the glands of *Drosophyllum*, *Pinguicula* and *Drosera* show that larger and more numerous Golgi vesicles are present in the cells during the period of secretion.[219] Experiments indicate that secretion of the capturing-mucilage in *Drosophyllum* is respiration-dependent,[218] and that the rate of secretion is affected by temperature.[219]

The familiar tentacles of the leaves of sundew, *Drosera* spp., may be considered as large stalked glands which are not entirely of epidermal origin. These structures have a multicellular stalk, containing a bundle of tracheids and a head with three or four layers of cells covered by a cuticle.[168] The functions suggested for these glands include water storage, the reception and transmission of stimuli, secretion of mucilage, enzymes and water, and the absorption of the products of digestion. Since it seems unlikely that the cells are active in all these different ways, this list perhaps serves to emphasize how little is known about the functions of many secretory structures—almost as little, indeed, as is known about the factors leading to their differentiation.

The pitchers of *Nepenthes* also possess several different kinds of glands, which seem to differ more in position and in their supposed function than in structure. Multicellular 'alluring' glands, of epidermal origin, are

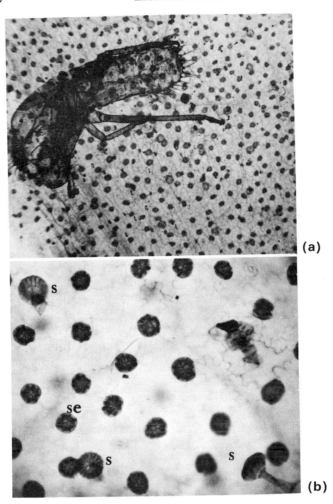

Fig. 10.2 Portions of cleared leaf of *Pinguicula vulgaris*. (a) Part of a leaf showing an insect victim that has been trapped by the hairs. × 40. (b) Enlarged view of part of the leaf surface, showing the sessile (se) and stalked (s) glandular hairs. The head of the stalked hairs is larger, and has 16 cells. × 120.

present on the under surface of the lid of the pitcher and elsewhere; they secrete nectar. Numerous digestive glands having the same structure are present on the inner surface of the pitcher wall, and glands with a possible digestive and absorptive function are present towards the base of the pitcher.[168]

The mechanism of the bladder-like traps of species of *Utricularia* (bladderwort) also depends on glandular structures. Stalked and sessile glands on the outside of the trap secrete mucilage and sugar, which may attract animals. Short-stalked glands on the inside of the bladders extract water from the contents, which creates a tension. If an animal then happens to touch the four stiff bristles on the outside of the door of the trap, it opens slightly, releasing the tension and causing an inrush of water. The victim passes in with the water and the door then closes again.[222]

Hydathodes

Hydathodes occur on leaves, and are usually associated with the marginal teeth or serrations, or the tip. They secrete water and discharge it in liquid form by a process known as guttation. In the case of the so-called active hydathodes, the energy involved in secretion is supplied by the glandular cells themselves. If the surface of the leaf is painted with an alcoholic solution of mercuric chloride, which kills the living cells of the hydathode, no liquid emerges from the treated hydathodes even if water is forced into the leaf under pressure.[129]

During the development of a hydathode procambium differentiates towards the lobes or serrations of the leaf, which may undergo some swelling. The cells adjacent to the procambium may proliferate to give rise to the *epithem*, a tissue of small, thin-walled, rather densely cytoplasmic cells with an extensive system of intercellular spaces. The cells of the epithem usually contain no chloroplasts,[250] unlike the adjacent mesophyll cells of the leaf. In the epidermis over-lying the epithem the mother cells of the water pores appear; these divide to give two guard cells, sometimes undergoing earlier divisions to give rise to subsidiary cells.[204] The guard cells of the water pores associated with hydathodes lose the power of controlling the aperture of the stoma. New water pores may form later between those already present. In some species, only one water pore is associated with each hydathode, but usually there are several and the number may be fairly constant within a particular species.

The cells of the epithem are in close contact with the terminal tracheary elements, usually tracheids, of the vein ending, and water moves through the numerous intercellular spaces of the epithem and is discharged through the open water pores. The hydathodes, perhaps especially those of aquatic plants, seem to function during only part of the life of the leaf.[186,250]

Nectaries

Nectaries are most commonly associated with parts of the flower, though the so-called 'extra-floral' nectaries may occur on stems or parts of leaves. They secrete nectar, a sugary fluid attractive to many insects. Dictyosomes are apparently not involved in the secretion of nectar[183] or of resin.[288] As in the case of hydathodes, tissue lying below the epidermis may be associated with the epidermis in forming the nectary. The cells of the nectary are usually densely cytoplasmic. Apparently passage of the nectar to the exterior may occur by diffusion through the cell walls, by rupture of the cuticle, or through stomata present in the epidermis.[105]

Studies with radioactive isotopes indicate that the cells of nectaries can not only secrete, but also absorb, a sugary fluid;[200] whether such a process occurs in nature appears doubtful. In the experiments the fluid applied was readily translocated to other parts of the plant; this ease of movement is undoubtedly linked with the fact that the vascular tissue associated with nectaries secreting a concentrated sugar solution may consist only, or predominantly, of phloem,[91] contrasting with the strands consisting entirely of xylem which are associated with hydathodes.

INTERNAL SECRETORY STRUCTURES

Secretion may be carried out internally by single cells, by small groups of cells, or by a whole tissue. Cells which secrete oils or enzymes may be distributed throughout a tissue, as in the endosperm of *Ricinus* and the cotyledons of *Arachis*, the sources of castor oil and ground nut (peanut) oil respectively. Other important oils are palm oil, extracted from the fleshy mesocarp of the fruit of *Elaeis guineensis*, and safflower oil, an unsaturated oil derived from the seeds of *Carthamus tinctorius*. In the shoot of *Ricinus*, secretory cells may differentiate in meristematic tissue at the apex, or much later, associated with secondary tissues.[31]

In some tissues, oil- or resin-secreting idioblasts occur. Examples of these are the oil cells in the phloem of *Cinnamomum zeylanicum*, which secrete the aromatic cinnamon oil, and the oleo-resin cells in the ground tissue of the rhizome of ginger, *Zingiber officinale*. Crystal-containing cells are also sometimes considered to have a secretory or excretory function. Occasionally, a whole layer of specialized secretory cells is present. For example, a layer of cells just within the testa secretes an aromatic oil in the seeds of cardamom, *Elettaria cardamomum*. The importance of the aleurone layer in the grains of cereals in secreting the enzyme α-amylase has already been discussed in Chapter 3.

Glands and ducts

In many instances small groups of thin-walled, densely protoplasmic cells which are a part of another tissue have a secretory function. Their secretions collect in an internal cavity, which may be more or less isodiametric

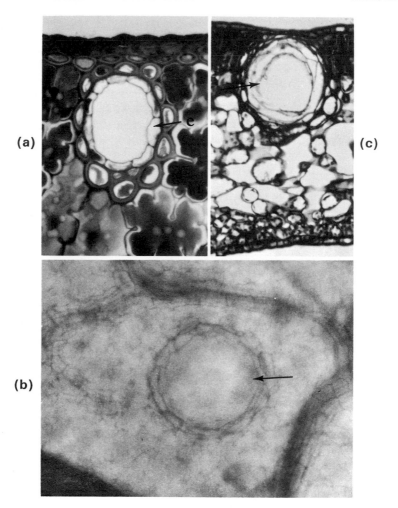

Fig. 10.3 Schizogenous and lysigenous secretory cavities. (a) Schizogenous resin duct from transverse section of leaf of *Pinus resinosa*. e, epithelium. × 300. (b) Transverse section of leaf of *Citrus* sp. with lysigenous oil gland. × 200. (c) Cleared leaf of *Citrus* sp., showing an oil gland in optical section. The views shown in **b** and **c** together demonstrate that the gland is isodiametric. × 200. In (b) and (c) the cells around the cavity which are undergoing lysis are arrowed.

(gland) or considerably elongated in one plane (duct). These cavities may originate either by a splitting apart of the cells at the middle lamella (schizogenous glands) or by actual breakdown or lysis of some of the cells (lysigenous glands). In some instances, schizogeny may be followed by lysis (schizolysigenous glands). In the case of schizogenous glands, a ring or lining of intact cells, the epithelium, surrounds the cavity, the boundary of which is well defined by their cell walls; lysigenous or schizolysigenous glands have no such clear-cut boundary.

The resin ducts of conifers and other genera are examples of schizogenous ducts (Fig. 10.3a). A study of the resin ducts of *Pinus* with the electron microscope[288] showed that the epithelial cells have many more relatively undifferentiated plastids than adjoining cortical cells. In the epithelial cells the plastids are sheathed with endoplasmic reticulum, and it is believed that this ER may play a role in transporting the resin to the duct. In conifers the ducts usually form a rather complex vertical and horizontal system within the plant, and may be branched. Resin ducts occur in species from many families, but only a few species have resins of commercial importance. Frankincense and myrrh are soft resins produced by members of the Burseraceae. In some plants, resin ducts apparently develop in response to injury, and wounding is consequently sometimes practised in the commercial collection of resins. The nature of the mechanism involved might be worthy of study with modern methods.

Lysigenous or schizolysigenous glands are present in the leaves and fruits of *Citrus* spp. (Fig. 10.3b, c). The glands occur, for example, in orange and lemon peel, in the outermost part of the pericarp. Schizolysigenous oil glands are also found in the floral parts of clove, *Eugenia caryophyllata*, and are the source of clove oil.

Laticifers

Perhaps the most important of all plant secretions is latex, a fluid secreted by specialized cells or groups of cells known as laticifers. Laticifers are unique among plant cells, and their structure and growth have many features of interest. Latex is found in representatives of about twenty plant families.[178]

Latex is most commonly milky white in colour, but may be clear and colourless, or yellow to orange. It may contain carbohydrates, organic acids, alkaloids, etc., in solution, and also various dispersed particles, including terpenes, oils, resins and rubber. Starch is also sometimes present. In *Euphorbia milii* the starch grains in the laticifers are elongated or dumb-bell shaped, whereas those in adjacent parenchyma cells are oval (Fig. 10.4). This raises the problem of how the starch is synthesized in both types of cell. The latex of *Carica papaya* is rich in the proteolytic enzyme papain,[274] and many other enzymes may be present in latex of other species.[9] The medically important alkaloid opium is present in the latex of *Papaver somniferum*. Small particles found in the latex of *Hevea* after centrifugation,

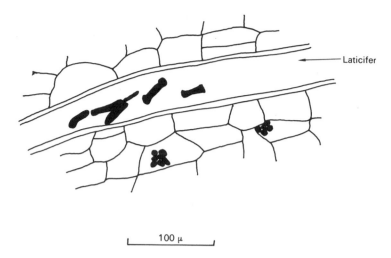

Fig. 10.4   Longitudinal section of stem of *Euphorbia milii*, showing the dumb-bell shaped starch grains in the laticifers, and the oval starch grains in adjacent parenchyma cells. Starch grains black.   × 230.

considered to be possibly a kind of plastid, suggest that latex is composed of cytoplasm rather than vacuolar sap.[234] Preliminary studies of the fine structure of the laticifers of *Achras sapota* reveal both electron-transparent organelles, which later degenerate, and electron-dense organelles, which constitute the main part of the latex.[212]

Laticifers may be divided into two main types, articulated and non-articulated. **Non-articulated laticifers** originate from single cells, which are apparently capable of potentially unlimited growth. By their continued growth these cells develop into long tube-like structures, which may branch but usually do not undergo anastomosis (Fig. 10.5). In *Nerium oleander*, the cells which will differentiate as laticifers become evident during the late globular stage of embryogeny. They appear in an irregular ring just below the corpus of the shoot apical meristem and differentiate from cells on the periphery of the future procambium.[174] Usually 28 such cells differentiate (Fig. 10.6). The laticifer initial cells grow more rapidly than neighbouring cells, and their nuclei also enlarge and subsequently divide without accompanying wall formation.

The developing non-articulated laticifer thus becomes a multinucleate cell; it is also characterized by extremely rapid growth. All mitotic figures are oriented in a plane approximately parallel to the long axis of the laticifer. There is a total absence of cell plate formation.[172] Many nuclei are usually present in the youngest part of the cell.[12] Apparently a wave of mitoses

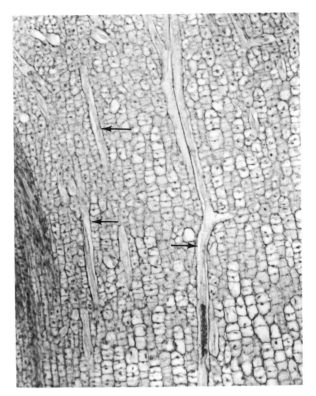

Fig. 10.5 Part of a longitudinal section of a shoot tip of *Nerium oleander*, slightly below the shoot apex, showing the non-articulated, branched laticifers (arrowed) ramifying through the tissue. × 150.

passes through the laticifer, so that nuclei are at successive stages of division along a region of the cell. This suggests that a mitotic stimulus may pass along the cell axis;[176] the nature of this stimulus is not known.

The non-articulated laticifers of *Nerium* branch repeatedly, and the laticifers of the shoot system are continuous with branches formed in the cotyledonary node of the embryo. These cells thus ramify through the tissues, by means of rapid and predominantly apical growth; the rate of growth of the various branches may not be uniform.[175] Laticifers grow intrusively, occupying the intercellular spaces, and apparently general cell elongation is involved as well as tip growth.[173] In some species, non-articulated laticifers are unbranched.

Laticifers usually have fairly thick walls, except at the extreme tip, thicker than those of neighbouring cells. The wall is formed by apposition,

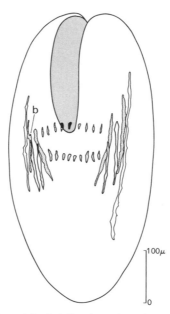

Fig. 10.6 Reconstruction of the laticifer tissue in an immature embryo of *Nerium oleander*. Twenty-eight laticifer initials of variable length are distributed along the periphery of the vascular tissue in the cotyledonary node. b indicates a branch. (From Mahlberg,[174] Fig. 1, p. 91.)

by a process of multi-net growth[184] (see Chapter 4). Experiments indicate that laticifers may have some mechanism for the closure of a wound—thus retaining the latex—but this may merely be coagulation of latex particles.[235]

Articulated laticifers are compound in origin, consisting of longitudinal files of cells, the end walls of which break down wholly or in part. In *Hevea brasiliensis*, the major source of rubber, laticiferous tubes or vessels occur associated with the phloem of the vascular bundles of the embryo in late development. Perforation of the lateral walls is apparently more advanced than that of the end walls, and a complex anastomosing system becomes established early in ontogeny.[220] In *Achras sapota*, disappearance of the end walls is also gradual.[151]

In *Papaver somniferum*, the opium poppy, laticifers are absent from the embryo and young seedling.[108] In *Taraxacum kok-saghyz*, also, laticifers are not present in the embryo, but differentiate in the pericycle of the primary root soon after germination. Resorption of the end walls occurs, and also lateral anastomosis.[11]

Laticifers may be fairly generally distributed in the tissues, but seem to be most commonly associated with the phloem. In *Taraxacum* root, the laticifers are located in the secondary phloem. Concentric cylinders of laticifers and sieve tube elements alternate with cylinders of parenchyma; no anastomoses take place between laticifers from different cylinders.[11] In *Hevea*, also, the main laticiferous system is in the secondary phloem.

ECONOMIC IMPORTANCE OF PLANT SECRETIONS

Many plant secretions are of commercial importance, but none more so than latex, because of the substances that it contains. Of these, rubber is the most important. The Indians of the Amazon region utilized rubber for making containers, balls for playing, etc., in quite early times; the earliest record is about 1510, but probably it was used considerably earlier.[274] The principal source of rubber is *Hevea brasiliensis*, which can yield about 2,000 lb rubber per acre per year; yields from *Taraxacum kok-saghyz* are only about 100 lb per acre per year, though yields of 400 lb have been reported.[9] 175 lb per acre can be obtained from *Cryptostegia grandiflora*.[178] The production of rubber in *Hevea* can be stimulated by application of hormones, and can also be affected by various minerals; in guayule (*Parthenium*), in which rubber occurs principally in the cells of the vascular rays, not in laticifers,[10] low night temperatures increased rubber production.[9] How these factors affect the physiology of the laticifers remains to be determined.

Gutta-percha is obtained by coagulating the latex of species of *Palaquium*. It has been used by the peoples of Borneo and neighbouring regions since early times to make containers and tools. At the present time it is employed in the manufacture, among other things, of dentures, golf balls, and underground and underwater cables; up to 1914, some 300,000 miles of submarine cable had been covered with gutta-percha.[282] The latex of another member of the same family (Sapotaceae), *Achras sapota*, is the original source of chicle, from which chewing gum is made. The importance of opium and its derivatives in medicine needs no emphasis.

Many oils secreted by plants are also of considerable economic value. Olive oil is widely used in a variety of ways. Safflower oil is becoming increasingly important, because of its unsaturated nature; it is utilized in the production of margarine and cooking oil. Palm oil is also used in margarine, as well as in the manufacture of soap and candles.

II

Vascular Cambium and Periderm

VASCULAR CAMBIUM

During the process of secondary growth a lateral meristem, the vascular cambium, comes to form a thin cylinder of cells surrounding the primary xylem in both the stems and roots of most dicotyledons and gymnosperms. The cylinder of cambial cells, once complete, divides predominantly periclinally, forming a cylinder of secondary phloem towards the outside of the organ, and a cylinder of secondary xylem towards the inside. The process of secondary growth in roots and stems is discussed in Part 2, Chapters 2 and 4.

The thin-walled cells of the vascular cambium are highly vacuolate and in this respect are unlike most other meristematic cells. Examination of cambium cells with the electron microscope confirms their highly vacuolate nature. Many ribosomes and dictyosomes, and well developed endoplasmic reticulum, are present.[236]

The cambium is made up of two kinds of cell, the *fusiform* and *ray initials*. The latter are almost isodiametric and constitute the radial system of the vascular cambium, their products differentiating as parenchymatous rays. The fusiform initials, the axial system of the cambium, are considerably elongated in the longitudinal plane of the axis and are approximately prism-shaped (Fig. 11.1). In some species the fusiform initials are arranged in regular rows, having a stratified structure, in others the cambium is non-stratified.

The fusiform initials of the cambium do not obey the usual laws of cell division. They usually divide vertically, in the longitudinal plane, thus contravening Errera's law, for example, which asserts that a cell will

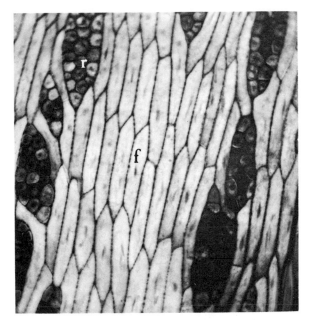

Fig. 11.1 Tangential longitudinal section through the cambial region of *Robinia pseudacacia*. The cambium is non-storied. f, fusiform initials; r, ray initials. ×200.

divide by a wall of minimal area. In the fusiform initial, a wall of minimal area would be transverse (horizontal). Divisions of this kind do occasionally occur, during the formation of additional ray initials, but are much less frequent than divisions resulting in a vertically oriented wall. Such divisions are mainly periclinal, but some anticlinal divisions also occur; the latter keep pace with the growth in girth of the stem or root. In longitudinal divisions the wall forms first in the region of the nucleus and grows towards the ends of the cell, which it may not reach for some time after mitosis.

By periclinal divisions of the fusiform initials, radially oriented files of cells are produced. Usually more xylem than phloem is formed. Towards the inside of the stem or root these cells differentiate to form the axial system of the secondary xylem; towards the outside they differentiate into the axial system of the secondary phloem. At certain seasons a fairly wide zone of undifferentiated cells is present between the secondary xylem and phloem; these cells constitute the cambial zone, but only one layer of true cambial initials is present. Cells produced by the ray initials differentiate as the parenchymatous vascular rays. The fine structure of the fusiform and ray initials of the cambium is similar,[236] and the basis for the differences in size and shape and in the fate of their products is not yet understood.

Since some specimens of *Sequoiadendron*, for example, are found to be 3,000 or 4,000 years old, the cambial initials are evidently capable of periods of intermittent but considerable activity more or less indefinitely. This virtual immortality of the cambial cells is one of their most interesting features. In perennial plants cambial activity is a seasonal phenomenon and occurs during the period of active growth, beginning in the spring. Considerable research has been directed towards elucidating the factors that stimulate the seasonal activity of the vascular cambium. Since organographic considerations are involved, discussion of this interesting work is deferred until Chapters 2 and 4 of Part 2. Suffice it to say here that various experiments have shown that auxin and gibberellin are among the factors that stimulate cambial activity.

It seems possible that cytokinins, usually considered to stimulate cell division, may also affect cambial activity. In cell suspension cultures derived from the cambium of *Acer*, kinetin increased cell number. The

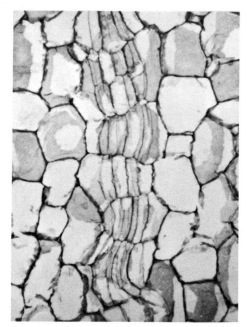

Fig. 11.2 Tangential longitudinal section through a stem of *Agave* in the cambial region. Two kinds of cells are present: squat, parenchymatous cells; and narrow, elongated cells, formed by division of the former, that will give rise to a vascular bundle. × 150.

highest rate of cell division was attained in the presence of auxin, gibberellin and kinetin together.[76]

In some monocotyledons, a type of vascular cambium is present in outer regions of the stem; it gives rise on the inner side to entire vascular bundles comprising both xylem and phloem, and on the outer side to parenchyma.[49] Very little is known about either the structure and functioning of this type of cambium, or the factors controlling its initiation and activity. The cells of the cambial region may be fusiform, rectangular or polygonal and may vary even in a single plant.[49] The occurrence of two kinds of cells in this tissue is illustrated in Fig. 11.2.

PERIDERM

The periderm is a protective tissue which usually replaces the outer tissues of stems and roots that undergo secondary thickening. It is formed by another lateral meristem, the *phellogen* or cork cambium. The cells of the phellogen are meristematic, but like those of the vascular cambium are highly vacuolate; however, unlike the vascular cambium, with its fusiform and ray initials, the cells of the phellogen are all of one kind. The phellogen divides periclinally to give radially seriate files of cells; those towards the outside differentiate as *phellem* or cork, those towards the inside as *phelloderm* or secondary cortex. When the phellogen is highly active, it gives rise to large, thin-walled phellem cells, in contrast to the flat cells with thicker walls formed by a less active meristem.[264]

The cells of the phellem or cork are dead at maturity, and have suberized cell walls. Suberin is a fatty substance, and it is this which makes the cork essentially impervious and confers upon it its protective properties. The cells of the phelloderm, formed towards the inside of the phellogen, are living and are often only distinguishable from the cortical cells by their radial alignment with the phellogen and phellem.

Like the vascular cambium, the phellogen gives rise to an unequal number of derivatives on either side during a growing season. The situation is the inverse of that in the vascular cambium, however, greater numbers of cells differentiating on the outer (phellem) side of the phellogen. Up to 20 rows of cork cells may be produced in a single season.

In some stems the inception and development of one phellogen may be followed by others. The later-formed phellogens are successively more deep-seated. Each phellogen functions normally and produces phellem and phelloderm. Pockets of tissue, usually secondary phloem, become isolated between the periderms, and these cells die. All of this tissue is sometimes referred to as *rhytidome* (Fig. 11.3). If the various phellogens form complete cylinders around the stem, a ring bark is formed; if they form separate arcs, a scale bark is formed.

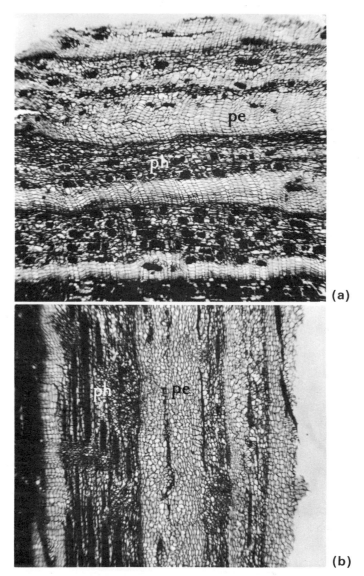

(a)

(b)

Fig. 11.3 (a) Transverse section and (b) longitudinal section of rhytidome in *Robinia pseudacacia*. Successive phellogens originate more and more deeply in the stem, giving rise to bands of suberized periderm (pe) which cut off and isolate regions of the secondary phloem (ph). These sections also show the isodiametric nature of the cells of the periderm.   × 40.

Bark is a more inclusive term than periderm; it includes all the tissues outside the vascular cambium, viz., secondary phloem, primary phloem, cortex, periderm and any tissues outside the periderm. Barks usually contain a quantity of sclerenchyma, including phloem fibres and often also sclereids. Indeed, barks are made up of a considerable variety of tissues, and their structure is very varied in different species.[90]

Certain regions of the periderm are differentiated as *lenticels* (Fig. 11.4).

Fig. 11.4   Transverse section of outer part of the stem of *Sambucus*, showing a lenticel. ct, complementary tissue.   × 60.

Some parts of the phellogen, usually below a stoma, and continuous with the rest of the phellogen, function rather differently and form a mass of unsuberized and loosely arranged cells called complementary tissue. In contrast to cork, in which no air spaces occur, many intercellular spaces are present in complementary tissue; lenticels are believed to function in gaseous exchange. The complementary tissue eventually breaks through the epidermis and may protrude.

Cork cells are dead and filled with air and function more or less as air cushions. Cork is resilient, resistant to pressure, impermeable to liquids and resistant to acids, organic solvents and many other chemicals.[60] All of these properties render it of considerable commercial importance. The chief source of cork is *Quercus suber*, the cork oak. The first cork formed is useless for commercial purposes, and this is stripped off. This wounding process stimulates the formation of another phellogen, and the whole process is repeated periodically.

In some monocotyledons a type of cork known as storied cork is formed. This does not originate from a true phellogen, but by successive periclinal divisions of parenchyma cells. Their derivatives are suberized and arranged in radial files.

Whitmore[280] has studied the strains that may be set up in phloem and in mature bark by the formation of secondary xylem and phloem. Differences in rates of growth of the phloem, calculated from measurements of total tangential growth in the bark and the xylem growth rate, seemed to be related causally to the surface pattern and structure of the bark in different species.[281]

Little is known about the factors leading to the formation of phellogen. A type of phellogen layer was induced to form in willow stems treated with naphthaleneacetic acid in lanolin,[164] but it is perhaps doubtful if this tissue was very normal. Combinations of daylength and temperature also had an effect on phellogen activity.[264] As already mentioned, the formation of a phellogen can sometimes be stimulated by wounding. Perhaps it might be worth considering whether the strains resulting from formation of secondary xylem and phloem and consequent increase in girth of the stem, discussed above, might be of some causal significance in the initiation or stimulation of phellogen. In this connection it is interesting to note that stems of *Robinia pseudacacia* show only one annual period of cambial

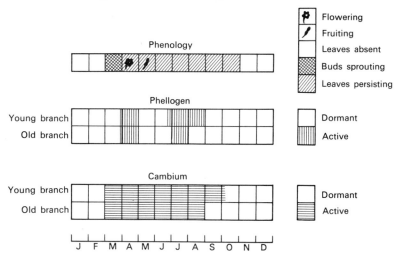

Fig. 11.5 Annual periods of activity of the phellogen and vascular cambium of young and old branches of a tree of *Robinia pseudacacia* growing outdoors in Tel-Aviv. (From Waisel, Liphschitz and Arzee,[264] Fig. 1, p. 333.)

activity, from about March to September (in Israel), whereas the phellogen shows two discontinuous periods of activity, approximately in April and in July–August (Fig. 11.5).[264] It seems possible, at least, to interpret these interesting observations in the following way: After the vascular cambium becomes active in March, the stem increases in girth, placing a strain on the tissues outside the vascular cylinder; this activates the phellogen, which functions during April and, by the production of periderm with accompanying radial divisions, relieves the strain and consequently ceases activity. Continued activity of the cambium, however, leads to renewed stimulation of the phellogen two months later, and the same sequence of events occurs. However, in subsequent work with *Robinia*[13a] no relationship was found between the xylem-bark ratio and the inception of phellogen. Treatment with gibberellic acid or naphthaleneacetic acid delayed the onset of phellogen activity to an older internode as compared with control plants. Since formation of phellogen was also retarded in long days and under conditions of high temperature, both of which stimulated extension growth, it is possible to speculate that phellogen formation may be inhibited by hormones produced by an actively growing shoot apex or other regions of the young shoot. Whatever the validity of such a speculation, this is possibly an interesting field for future experimental work.

Appendix

CLASS EXPERIMENT

The following experiment has been adapted from published work,* in consultation with the original authors, for class use. Detailed instructions are given.

The role of auxin in the regeneration of phloem and xylem in *Coleus*

Rooted cuttings of *Coleus* sp. about 8–10 weeks old are satisfactory material; avoid plants with abundant anthocyanin. Determine which is the fifth pair of expanded (i.e. clearly visible) leaves below the tip of the shoot. A wound will be made in one flat surface of the internode below this pair of leaves, designated the No. 5 internode.

Each student or pair of students requires three plants as comparable as possible and should undertake the following treatments:

(1) Make a small incision in the No. 5 internode, but otherwise leave the plant intact. A small scalpel should be inserted in the middle of one of the flat sides of the internode, in order to sever the fairly small central vascular bundle (larger bundles are present at the angles of the stem). The wound should be approximately 2–3 mm deep and 1–2 mm wide. (*Warning*: do not make the wound too large.) Ideally, the treatment should be performed in a darkened room with the stem illuminated from behind, in order to reveal the silhouette of the vascular bundle to be severed, but this is not essential.

(2) Make a wound in the No. 5 internode, as above, remove all leaves and buds from the stem below the wound, and from node No. 5 above the wound, and decapitate the plant some mm above node No. 5. You are left with a bare stem, wounded in the uppermost remaining internode. Treat the cut stump of stem with plain lanolin paste.†

---

* These details are taken from papers by LaMotte and Jacobs[159,160] and Thompson and Jacobs;[257] I am indebted to Dr. W. P. Jacobs and Dr. N. P. Thompson for additional information.

† To make the lanolin paste, weigh out between 50 and 60 g anhydrous lanolin in a beaker. Place in an oven at about 60°C overnight; it will now be melted, and a

(3) Proceed as for (2), but treat the cut stump of stem with lanolin paste containing 1% indoleacetic acid (IAA).*

After treatment allow the plants to grow (preferably in a greenhouse or growth chamber) for seven days. Then remove the wounded internode from the plant by a horizontal cut at its base and an oblique cut at its top, so that the apical end can later be identified. Remove the side of the internode opposite the wound with a razor blade, and fix the internode in Craf III. Leave for 24 hr (or longer); rinse in water. Then place the tissue in 85% lactic acid for 12–24 hr, to harden (this can also be left for longer, if necessary). Pour the lactic acid with the internode into a petri dish. Place the internode with the wounded side down and the side previously exposed with the razor blade uppermost, and observe it under a dissecting microscope. Peel back the right (R) and left (L) sides with a blunt dissecting needle, holding the internode with a spatula or similar instrument. Now hold the peeled-back L side with the spatula and roll the central cylinder of the stem, comprising xylem and pith, towards the R side with the dissecting needle. The wounded strip (on the lowermost side) should thus become cleanly separated from the inner tissues. (N.B. The phloem should remain attached to this strip. If separating does not occur in this way, start rolling the central cylinder again from the opposite side.) The R and L sides should now be cut off, leaving only the wounded strip of tissue. (*Warning*: do not cut off too much of the sides.)

For phloem

Transfer the strips with the phloem attached to 0·1% aniline blue in 85% lactic acid for 6–12 hr. (If it is not convenient to proceed with this at this stage, the phloem strips can be left in 85% lactic acid.) After staining in aniline blue, transfer to 60% alcohol containing 0·5% HCl and peel off the epidermis, scar tissue and cortex with fine forceps under a dissecting microscope. (This is difficult, and it may prove expedient to leave some of this tissue still attached. If left too long in the acid alcohol, the tissue will destain more or less completely.) Stain the remaining thin strips again with aniline blue–lactic acid, and pass them through two changes (each for about 10 min, especially if the pieces of tissue are still fairly thick) of acidified 60% alcohol, two changes of absolute alcohol and two of xylol. Mount in canada balsam. Apply weights to the cover slips and keep the slides warm for several days.

---

deep yellow colour. Add water to make 100 g, stirring vigorously. During this process the hydrated lanolin will turn almost white. Dissolve 1·0 g IAA in a little absolute alcohol and add this to the hydrated lanolin, stirring very vigorously to ensure thorough mixing. Make up the control plain lanolin paste without IAA, but with an equivalent quantity of absolute alcohol. Store in a refrigerator, removing some hours before use.

* See previous footnote.

For xylem

After the strip with the phloem, cortex and epidermis has been peeled from the remainder of the stem, rinse the remaining cylinder of xylem and pith in water for about an hour. Then place the cylinder for 1–2 hr (less will do) in concentrated ammonium hydroxide which has been saturated with basic fuchsin. (To make the fuchsin–ammonia solution add a saturated aqueous solution of basic fuchsin to ammonia until a yellow or brownish ('straw') colour is obtained. It is better to do this under a hood.) Now pour off the ammonia solution and rinse the cylinders several times with water; allow them to remain in water until the vascular bundles appear red. It may be beneficial to leave the cylinders in water overnight, since they become too red if subsequent dehydration is begun too soon after the bundles are red.

Place the cylinders in a petri dish containing water under a dissecting microscope with the wounded side of the stem down. With a sharp scalpel, cut the xylem from the pith on the R and L sides of the cylinder. Now the xylem tissue should be free from the pith on sides adjacent to the wounded side but still attached on the wounded side. Gently cut off the pith from the xylem on the wounded side, gradually, with care. When the pith has been removed, cut away part of the xylem on the R and L sides, leaving part of each corner bundle with the wounded side (do not cut away too much of the xylem from the sides). Scrape away remaining pith from the wounded side and place the xylem in 50% alcohol. Pass the tissue through an alcohol-xylol series, leaving it about 10 min in each solution, and mount it pith side down on a slide. Mount in canada balsam. Again apply weights to the cover slips and keep the slides warm for several days.

Further Reading

CARLQUIST, S. (1961). *Comparative Plant Anatomy.* Holt, Rinehart and Winston, New York.

EAMES, A. J. and MACDANIELS, L. H. (1947). *An Introduction to Plant Anatomy.* 2nd edition. McGraw-Hill, New York and London.

ESAU, K. (1960). *Anatomy of Seed Plants.* Wiley, New York.

ESAU, K. (1965). *Plant Anatomy.* 2nd edition. Wiley, New York.

FAHN, A. (1967). *Plant Anatomy.* (Translated from the Hebrew by Sybil Broido-Altman). Pergamon Press, Oxford.

FOSTER, A. S. (1949). *Practical Plant Anatomy.* 2nd edition. Van Nostrand, New York.

METCALFE, C. R. (1960). *Anatomy of the Monocotyledons. I. Gramineae.* Clarendon Press, Oxford.

METCALFE, C. R. and CHALK, L. (1950). *Anatomy of the Dicotyledons.* Vols. I and II. Clarendon Press, Oxford.

TOMLINSON, P. B. (1961). *Anatomy of the Monocotyledons. II. Palmae.* Clarendon Press, Oxford.

WARDLAW, C. W. (1968). *Morphogenesis in Plants.* Methuen, London.

References

1. AJELLO, L. (1941). Cytology and cellular interrelations of cystolith formation in *Ficus elastica*. *Am. J. Bot.*, **28**, 589–594.
2. ALDABA, V. C. (1927). The structure and development of the cell wall in plants. I. Bast fibers of *Boehmeria* and *Linum*. *Am. J. Bot.*, **14**, 16–24.
3. ALLDRIDGE, N. A. (1964). Anomalous vessel elements in wilty-dwarf tomato. *Bot. Gaz.*, **125**, 138–142.
4. AL-TALIB, K. H. and TORREY, J. G. (1959). The aseptic culture of isolated buds of *Pseudotsuga taxifolia*. *Pl. Physiol.*, *Lancaster*, **34**, 630–637.
5. AL-TALIB, K. H. and TORREY, J. G. (1961). Sclereid distribution in the leaves of *Pseudotsuga* under natural and experimental conditions. *Am. J. Bot.*, **48**, 71–79.
6. ARIYANAYAGAM, D. V. and STEBBINS, G. L. (1962). Developmental studies of cell differentiation in the epidermis of monocotyledons. III. Interaction of environmental and genetic factors on stomatal differentiation in three genotypes of barley. *Devl Biol.*, **4**, 117–133.
7. ARNOTT, H. J. and PAUTARD, F. G. E. (1965a). Mineralization in plants. (Abstr.) *Am. J. Bot.*, **52**, 613.
8. ARNOTT, H. J. and PAUTARD, F. G. E. (1965b). Development of raphide idioblasts in *Lemna*. (Abstr.) *Am. J. Bot.*, **52**, 618–619.
9. ARREGUÍN, B. (1958). Rubber and latex. *Handb. PflPhysiol.*, **10**, 223–248.
10. ARTSCHWAGER, E. (1943a). Contribution to the morphology and anatomy of guayule (*Parthenium argentatum*). *Tech. Bull. U.S. Dep. Agric.*, **842**. (33 pp.).
11. ARTSCHWAGER, E. (1943b). Contribution to the morphology and anatomy of the Russian Dandelion (*Taraxacum koksaghyz*). *Tech. Bull. U.S. Dep. Agric.*, **843**. (24 pp.).
12. ARTSCHWAGER, E. (1946). Contribution to the morphology and anatomy of cryptostegia (*Cryptostegia grandiflora*). *Tech. Bull. U.S. Dep. Agric.*, **915**. (40 pp.).
13. ARZEE, T. (1953). Morphology and ontogeny of foliar sclereids in *Olea europaea*. I. Distribution and structure. II. Ontogeny. *Am. J. Bot.*, **40**, 680–687 and 745–752.
13a. ARZEE, T., LIPHSCHITZ, N. and WAISEL, Y. (1968). The origin and development of the phellogen in *Robinia pseudacacia* L. *New Phytol.*, **67**, 87–93.
14. ASH, A. L. (1948). Hemp—production and utilization. *Econ. Bot.*, **2**, 158–169.

15. ATAL, C. K. (1961). Effect of gibberellin on the fibers of hemp. *Econ. Bot.*, **15**, 133–139.
16. AVERS, C. J. (1958). Histochemical localization of enzyme activity in the root epidermis of *Phleum pratense*. *Am. J. Bot.*, **45**, 609–613.
17. AVERS, C. J. (1961). Histochemical localization of enzyme activities in root meristem cells. *Am. J. Bot.*, **48**, 137–143.
18. AVERS, C. J. (1963). Fine structure studies of *Phleum* root meristem cells. II. Mitotic asymmetry and cellular differentiation. *Am. J. Bot.*, **50**, 140–148.
19. AVERS, C. J. and GRIMM, R. B. (1959). Comparative enzyme differentiation in grass roots. I. Acid phosphatase. *Am. J. Bot.*, **46**, 190–193.
20. BAILEY, I. W. (1957). The potentialities and limitations of wood anatomy in the study of the phylogeny and classification of angiosperms. *J. Arnold Arbor.*, **38**, 243–254.
21. BAILEY, I. W. (1964). *Contributions to Plant Anatomy*. Chronica Botanica, Waltham, Mass.
22. BAKER, H. G. (1965). *Plants and Civilization*. Wadsworth, Belmont, California.
23. BEER, M. and SETTERFIELD, G. (1958). Fine structure in thickened primary walls of collenchyma cells of celery petioles. *Am. J. Bot.*, **45**, 571–580.
24. BELFORD, D. S. and PRESTON, R. D. (1961). The structure and growth of root hairs. *J. exp. Bot.*, **12**, 157–168.
25. BELL, P. R. (1965). The structure and origin of mitochondria. *Sci. Progr., Lond.*, **53**, 33–44.
26. BIERHORST, D. W. and ZAMORA, P. M. (1965). Primary xylem elements and element associations of angiosperms. *Am. J. Bot.*, **52**, 657–710.
27. BISALPUTRA, T. and ESAU, K. (1964). Polarized light study of phloem differentiation in embryo of *Chenopodium album*. *Bot. Gaz.*, **125**, 1–7.
28. BLAKELY, L. M. and STEWARD, F. C. (1964). Growth and organized development of cultured cells. V. The growth of colonies from free cells on nutrient agar. *Am. J. Bot.*, **51**, 780–791.
29. BLOCH, R. (1944). Developmental potency, differentiation and pattern in meristems of *Monstera deliciosa*. *Am. J. Bot.*, **31**, 71–77.
30. BLOCH, R. (1946). Differentiation and pattern in *Monstera deliciosa*. The idioblastic development of the trichosclereids in the air root. *Am. J. Bot.*, **33**, 544 551.
31. BLOCH, R. (1948). The development of the secretory cells of *Ricinus* and the problem of cellular differentiation. *Growth*, **12**, 271–284.
32. BLOCH, R. (1965). Histological foundations of differentiation and development in plants. *Handb. PflPhysiol.*, **15**, 1, 146–188.
33. BONNER, J. (1965). *The Molecular Biology of Development*. Cambridge University Press, London.
34. BONNETT, H. T., Jr. and NEWCOMB, E. H. (1965). Polyribosomes and cisternal accumulations in root cells of radish. *J. Cell Biol.*, **27**, 423–432.
35. BOUCK, G. B. (1963a). Stratification and subsequent behavior of plant cell organelles. *J. Cell Biol.*, **18**, 441–457.
36. BOUCK, G. B. (1963b). An examination of the effects of ultracentrifugation on the organelles in living root tip cells. *Am. J. Bot.*, **50**, 1046–1054.
37. BOUCK, G. B. and CRONSHAW, J. (1965). The fine structure of differentiating sieve tube elements. *J. Cell Biol.*, **25**, 79–95.

146   REFERENCES

38. BROWN, R. (1958). Cellular basis for the induction of morphological structures. *Nature, Lond.*, **181**, 1546–1547.
39. BROWN, W. V. and JOHNSON, SR. C. (1962). The fine structure of the grass guard cell. *Am. J. Bot.*, **49**, 110–115.
40. BÜNNING, E. (1952). Morphogenesis in plants. *Surv. biol. Prog.*, **2**, 105–140.
41. BÜNNING, E. (1957). Polarität und inaquale Teilung des pflanzlichen Protoplasten. *Protoplasmatologia*, **8**, 1–86.
42. BÜNNING, E. (1965). Die Entstehung von Mustern in der Entwicklung von Pflanzen. *Handb. PflPhysiol.*, **15**, 1, 383–408.
43. BÜNNING, E. and BIEGERT, F. (1953). Die Bildung der Spaltöffnungs-initialen bei *Allium Cepa*. *Z. Bot.*, **41**, 17–39.
44. BÜNNING, E. and SAGROMSKY, H. (1948). Die Bildung des Spaltöffnungs-musters in der Blattepidermis. *Z. Naturf.*, 3b, 203–216.
45. BUTTROSE, M. (1963). Ultrastructure of the developing aleurone cells of wheat grain. *Aust. J. biol. Sci.*, **16**, 768–774.
46. BUVAT, R. (1963). Sur la présence d'acide ribonucléique dans les 'corpuscules muqueux' des cellules criblées de *Cucurbita pepo*. *C. r. hebd. Séanc. Acad. Sci., Paris*, **257**, 733–735.
47. CAMUS, G. (1943). Sur le greffage de bourgeons d'Endive sur des fragments de tissus cultivés in vitro. *C. r. Séanc. Soc. Biol.*, **137**, 184–185.
48. CARLQUIST, S. (1961). *Comparative Plant Anatomy*. Holt, Rinehart and Winston, New York.
49. CHEADLE, V. I. (1937). Secondary growth by means of a thickening ring in certain monocotyledons. *Bot. Gaz.*, **98**, 535–555.
50. CHEADLE, V. I. (1956). Research on xylem and phloem—progress in fifty years. *Am. J. Bot.*, **43**, 719–731.
51. CHEADLE, V. I. (1963). Vessels in Iridaceae. *Phytomorphology*, **13**, 245–248.
52. CHEADLE, V. I. and ESAU, K. (1958). Secondary phloem of Calycanthaceae. *Univ. Calif. Publs Bot.*, **29**, 397–510.
53. CHEADLE, V. I. and TUCKER, J. (1961). Vessels and phylogeny of Mono-cotyledoneae. In *Recent Advances in Botany*, 161–165. Toronto University Press.
54. CHEADLE, V. I. and WHITFORD, N. B. (1941). Observations on the phloem in Monocotyledoneae. I. The occurrence and phylogenetic special-ization in structure of the sieve tubes in the metaphloem. *Am. J. Bot.*, **28**, 623–627.
55. CLUTTER, M. E. (1960). Hormonal induction of vascular tissue in tobacco pith in vitro. *Science, N. Y.*, **132**, 548–549.
56. CLUTTER, M. E. (1963). Effects of IAA and kinetin on cell differentiation in cabbage pith cultures. *Pl. Physiol., Lancaster*, **38** (Suppl.), xii.
57. COBLEY, L. S. (1956). *An Introduction to the Botany of Tropical Crops*. Longmans, Green, London.
58. COMMONER, B. and ZUCKER, M. L. (1953). Cellular differentiation: an experimental approach. In *Growth and Differentiation in Plants*, 339–392. Iowa State College Press, Ames, Iowa.
59. CONWAY, V. M. (1937). Studies on the autecology of *Cladium mariscus* R. Br. III. The aeration of the subterranean parts of the plant. *New Phytol.*, **36**, 64–96.
60. COOKE, G. B. (1948). Cork and cork products. *Econ. Bot.*, **2**, 393–402.

61. CORMACK, R. G. H. (1937). The development of root hairs by *Elodea canadensis*. *New Phytol.*, **36**, 19–25.
62. CORMACK, R. G. H. (1949). The development of root hairs in angiosperms. *Bot. Rev.*, **15**, 583–612.
63. CORMACK, R. G. H. (1962). Development of root hairs in angiosperms. II. *Bot. Rev.*, **28**, 446–464.
64. COWAN, J. M. (1950). *The Rhododendron Leaf.* Oliver and Boyd, Edinburgh.
65. CRAFTS, A. S. and CURRIER, H. B. (1963). On sieve tube function. *Protoplasma*, **57**, 188–202.
66. CRONSHAW, J. (1967). Tracheid differentiation in tobacco pith cultures. *Planta*, **72**, 78–90.
67. CRONSHAW, J. and BOUCK, G. B. (1965). The fine structure of differentiating xylem elements. *J. Cell Biol.*, **24**, 415–431.
68. CRONSHAW, J. and ESAU, K. (1967). Tubular and fibrillar components of mature and differentiating sieve elements. *J. Cell Biol.*, **34**, 801–815.
69. CRÜGER, H. (1855). Zur Entwicklungsgeschichte der Zellenwand. *Bot. Ztg*, **13**, 601–613 and 617–629.
70. CUTTER, E. G. (1967). Differentiation of trichoblasts in roots of *Hydrocharis*. (Abstr.) *Am. J. Bot.*, **54**, 632.
71. CUTTER, E. G. (1970). *Plant Anatomy: Experiment and Interpretation.* Part 2: *Organs.* Edward Arnold, London (in preparation).
72. CZERNIK, C. A. and AVERS, C. J. (1964). Phosphatase activity and cellular differentiation in *Phleum* root meristem. *Am. J. Bot.*, **51**, 424–431.
73. DALE, H. M. (1951). Carbon dioxide and root hair development in *Anacharis* (*Elodea*). *Science, N. Y.*, **114**, 438–439.
74. DAWES, C. J. and BOWLER, E. (1959). Light and electron microscope studies of the cell wall structure of the root hairs of *Raphanus sativus*. *Am. J. Bot.*, **46**, 561–565.
75. DEMAGGIO, A., WETMORE, R. and MOREL, G. (1963). Induction de tissu vasculaire dans le prothalle de Fougère. *C. r. Séanc. Acad. Sci., Paris*, **256**, 5196–5199.
76. DIGBY, J. and WAREING, P. F. (1966). The effect of growth hormones on cell division and expansion in liquid suspension cultures of *Acer pseudoplatanus*. *J. exp. Bot.*, **17**, 718–725.
77. DORMER, K. J. (1961). The crystals in the ovaries of certain Compositae. *Ann. Bot., N. S.*, **25**, 241–254.
78. DORMER, K. J. (1962). The taxonomic significance of crystal forms in *Centaurea*. *New Phytol.*, **61**, 32–35.
79. DRIESCH, H. (1908). *The Science and Philosophy of the Organism.* A. & C. Black, London.
80. DUCHAIGNE, A. (1955). Les divers types de collenchymes chez les Dicotylédones; leur ontogénie et leur lignification. *Annls Sci. nat., Bot.*, sér. 11, **16**, 455–479.
81. ENGLEMAN, E. M. (1965a). Sieve element of *Impatiens sultanii*. 1. Wound reaction. *Ann. Bot., N.S.*, **29**, 83–101.
82. ENGLEMAN, E. M. (1965b). Sieve element of *Impatiens sultanii*. 2. Developmental aspects. *Ann. Bot., N.S.*, **29**, 103–118.
83. ERICKSON, R. O. (1961). Probability of division of cells in the epidermis of the *Phleum* root. *Am. J. Bot.*, **48**, 268–274.
84. ESAU, K. (1936a). Ontogeny and structure of collenchyma and of vascular tissues in celery petioles. *Hilgardia*, **10**, 431–476.

85. ESAU, K. (1936b). Vessel development in celery. *Hilgardia*, **10**, 479–484.
86. ESAU, K. (1943). Vascular differentiation in the vegetative shoot of *Linum*. III. The origin of the bast fibers. *Am. J. Bot.*, **30**, 579–586.
87. ESAU, K. (1948). Phloem structure in the grapevine, and its seasonal changes. *Hilgardia*, **18**, 217–296.
88. ESAU, K. (1961). *Plants, Viruses, and Insects*. Harvard University Press, Cambridge, Mass.
89. ESAU, K. (1964a). Aspects of ultrastructure of phloem. In *The Formation of Wood in Forest Trees*, Zimmermann, M. H., 51–63. Academic Press, New York.
90. ESAU, K. (1964b). Structure and development of the bark in dicotyledons. In *The Formation of Wood in Forest Trees*, Zimmermann, M. H., 37–50. Academic Press, New York.
91. ESAU, K. (1965a). *Plant Anatomy*. 2nd edition. Wiley, New York.
92. ESAU, K. (1965b). *Vascular Differentiation in Plants*. Holt, Rinehart and Winston, New York.
93. ESAU, K. and CHEADLE, V. I. (1958). Wall thickening in sieve elements. *Proc. natn. Acad. Sci. U.S.A.*, **44**, 546–553.
94. ESAU, K. and CHEADLE, V. I. (1959). Size of pores and their content in sieve elements of dicotyledons. *Proc. natn. Acad. Sci. U.S.A.*, **45**, 156–162.
95. ESAU, K. and CHEADLE, V. I. (1961). An evaluation of studies on ultrastructure of sieve plates. *Proc. natn. Acad. Sci. U.S.A.*, **47**, 1716–1726.
96. ESAU, K. and CHEADLE, V. I. (1962). Mitochondria in the phloem of *Cucurbita*. *Bot. Gaz.*, **124**, 79–85.
97. ESAU, K. and CHEADLE, V. I. (1965). Cytologic studies on phloem. *Univ. Calif. Publs Bot.*, **36**, 253–344.
98. ESAU, K., CHEADLE, V. I. and GILL, R. H. (1966a). Cytology of differentiating tracheary elements. I. Organelles and membrane systems. *Am. J. Bot.*, **53**, 756–764.
99. ESAU, K., CHEADLE, V. I. and GILL, R. H. (1966b). Cytology of differentiating tracheary elements. II. Structures associated with cell surfaces. *Am. J. Bot.*, **53**, 765–771.
100. ESAU, K., CHEADLE, V. I. and RISLEY, E. B. (1962). Development of sieve-plate pores. *Bot. Gaz.*, **123**, 233–243.
101. ESAU, K., CHEADLE, V. I. and RISLEY, E. B. (1963). A view of ultrastructure of *Cucurbita* xylem. *Bot. Gaz.*, **124**, 311–316.
102. ESAU, K., CURRIER, H. B. and CHEADLE, V. I. (1957). Physiology of phloem. *A. Rev. Pl. Physiol.*, **8**, 349–374.
103. ESCHRICH, W. (1953). Beiträge zur Kenntniss der Wundsiebröhrenentwicklung bei *Impatiens Holsti*. *Planta*, **43**, 37–74.
104. EVERT, R. F. and KOZLOWSKI, T. T. (1967). Effect of isolation of bark on cambial activity and development of xylem and phloem in trembling aspen. *Am. J. Bot.*, **54**, 1045–1055.
105. FAHN, A. (1952). On the structure of floral nectaries. *Bot. Gaz.*, **113**, 464–470.
106. FAHN, A. and ARNON, N. (1963). The living wood fibres of *Tamarix aphylla* and the changes occurring in them in transition from sapwood to heartwood. *New Phytol.*, **62**, 99–104.
107. FAHN, A. and LESHEM, B. (1963). Wood fibres with living protoplasts. *New Phytol.*, **62**, 91–98.

108. FAIRBAIRN, J. W. and KAPOOR, L. D. (1960). The laticiferous vessels of *Papaver somniferum* L. *Planta med.*, **8**, 49–61.

109. FLORIN, R. (1933). Studien über die Cycadales des Mesozoikums nebst Erörterungen über die Spaltöffnungs apparate der Bennettitales. *K. svenska VetenskAkad. Handl.*, ser. 3, **12**.

110. FOARD, D. E. (1958). An experimental study of sclereid development in the leaf of *Camellia japonica*. *Pl. Physiol., Lancaster*, **33** (Suppl.), xli.

111. FOARD, D. E. (1959). Pattern and control of sclereid formation in the leaf of *Camellia japonica*. *Nature, Lond.*, **184**, 1663–1664.

112. FOARD, D. E. and HABER, A. H. (1961). Anatomic studies of gamma-irradiated wheat growing without cell division. *Am. J. Bot.*, **48**, 438–446.

113. FOARD, D. E., HABER, A. H. and FISHMAN, T. N. (1965). Initiation of lateral root primordia without completion of mitosis and without cyto-kinesis in uniseriate pericycle. *Am. J. Bot.*, **52**, 580–590.

114. FOSKET, D. E. and ROBERTS, L. W. (1964). Induction of wound-vessel differentiation in isolated *Coleus* stem segments in vitro. *Am. J. Bot.*, **51**, 19–25.

115. FOSTER, A. S. (1947). Structure and ontogeny of the terminal sclereids in the leaf of *Mouriria Huberi* Cogn. *Am. J. Bot.*, **34**, 501–514.

116. FOSTER, A. S. (1949). *Practical Plant Anatomy*. 2nd edition. Van Nostrand, New York.

117. FOSTER, A. S. (1955). Structure and ontogeny of terminal sclereids in *Boronia serrulata*. *Am. J. Bot.*, **42**, 551–560.

118. FRANKE, W. (1961). Ectodesmata and foliar absorption. *Am. J. Bot.*, **48**, 683–691.

119. FREY-WYSSLING, A., and MÜHLETHALER, K. (1965). *Ultrastructural Plant Cytology*. Elsevier, Amsterdam, London, New York.

120. GAUDET, J. (1960). Ontogeny of foliar sclereids in *Nymphaea odorata*. *Am. J. Bot.*, **47**, 525–532.

121. GEESTERANUS, R. A. M. (1941). On the development of the stellate form of the pith cells of *Juncus* species. *Proc. K. ned. Akad. Wet.*, **44**, 489–501 and 648–653.

122. GOODWIN, R. H. (1942). On the development of xylary elements in the first internode of *Avena* in dark and light. *Am. J. Bot.*, **29**, 818–828.

123. GRAHAM, J. S. D., JENNINGS, A. C., MORTON, R. K., PALK, B. A. and RAISON, J. K. (1962). Protein bodies and protein synthesis in developing wheat endosperm. *Nature, Lond.*, **196**, 967–969.

124. GRANICK, S. (1961). The chloroplasts: inheritance, structure, and function. In *The Cell*, Vol. II, BRACHET, J. and MIRSKY, A. E., 489–619. Academic Press, New York and London.

125. GREW, N. (1682). *The Anatomy of Plants*. Johnson Reprint Corp., New York and London, 1965.

126. GROBSTEIN, C. (1966). What we do not know about differentiation. *Am. Zoologist*, **6**, 89–95.

127. HABER, A. H. (1962). Nonessentiality of concurrent cell divisions for degree of polarization of leaf growth. I. Studies with radiation-induced mitotic inhibition. *Am. J. Bot.*, **49**, 583–589.

128. HABER, A. H. and FOARD, D. E. (1963). Nonessentiality of concurrent cell divisions for degree of polarization of leaf growth. II. Evidence from untreated plants and from chemically induced changes of the degree of polarization. *Am. J. Bot.*, **50**, 937–944.

129. HABERLANDT, G. (1914). *Physiological Plant Anatomy*. Macmillan, London.
130. HALL, D. M. (1967). Wax microchannels in the epidermis of white clover. *Science, N. Y.*, **158**, 505–506.
131. HALPERIN, W. (1966). Alternative morphogenetic events in cell suspensions. *Am. J. Bot.*, **53**, 443–453.
132. HALPERIN, W. and JENSEN, W. A. (1967). Ultrastructural changes during growth and embryogenesis in carrot cell cultures. *J. Ultrastruct. Res.*, **18**, 428–443.
133. HARRIS, T. M. (1956). The fossil plant cuticle. *Endeavour*, **15**, 210–214.
134. HEPLER, P. K. and NEWCOMB, E. H. (1963). The fine structure of young tracheary xylem elements arising by redifferentiation of parenchyma in wounded *Coleus* stem. *J. exp. Bot.*, **14**, 496–503.
135. HEPLER, P. K. and NEWCOMB, E. H. (1964). Microtubules and fibrils in the cytoplasm of *Coleus* cells undergoing secondary wall deposition. *J. Cell Biol.*, **20**, 529–533.
136. HEPTON, C. E. L. and PRESTON, R. D. (1960). Electron microscopic observations of the structure of sieve-connexions in the phloem of angiosperms and gymnosperms. *J. exp. Bot.*, **11**, 381–394.
137. HESLOP-HARRISON, J. (1967). Differentiation. *A. Rev. Pl. Physiol.*, **18**, 325–348.
138. HOWE, K. J. and STEWARD, F. C. (1962). Anatomy and development of *Mentha piperita* L. *Mem. Cornell Univ. agric. Exp. Stn*, **379**, 11–40.
139. HULBARY, R. L. (1944). The influence of air spaces on the three-dimensional shapes of cells in *Elodea* stems, and a comparison with pith cells of *Ailanthus*. *Am. J. Bot.*, **31**, 561–580.
140. JACOBS, W. P. (1952). The role of auxin in differentiation of xylem around a wound. *Am. J. Bot.*, **39**, 301–309.
141. JACOBS, W. P. (1954). Acropetal auxin transport and xylem regeneration —a quantitative study. *Am. Nat.*, **88**, 327–337.
142. JACOBS, W. P. (1956). Internal factors controlling cell differentiation in the flowering plants. *Am. Nat.*, **90**, 163–169.
143. JACOBS, W. P. and MORROW, I. B. (1957). A quantitative study of xylem development in the vegetative shoot apex of *Coleus*. *Am. J. Bot.*, **44**, 823–842.
144. JACOBS, W. P. and MORROW, I. B. (1958). Quantitative relations between stages of leaf development and differentiation of sieve tubes. *Science, N. Y.*, **128**, 1084–1085.
145. JENNINGS, J. D. (1957). Danger Cave. *Anthrop. Pap. Univ. Utah*, **27**, 1–328.
146. JENSEN, W. A. (1961). Relation of primary cell wall formation to cell development in plants. In *Synthesis of Molecular and Cellular Structure*, RUDNICK, D. (Symp. Dev. Growth, **19**), 89–110.
147. JENSEN, W. A. (1964a). *The Plant Cell*. Wadsworth, Belmont, California.
148. JENSEN, W. A. (1964b). Cell development during plant embryogenesis. *Brookhaven Symp. Biol.*, **16**, 179–202.
149. JUNIPER, B. E. (1959). Growth, development, and effect of the environment on the ultra-structure of plant surfaces. *J. Linn. Soc. (Bot.)*, **56**, 413–419.
150. JUNIPER, B. E. and ROBERTS, R. M. (1966). Polysaccharide synthesis and the fine structure of root cells. *Jl R. microsc. Soc.*, **85**, 63–72.

151. KARLING, J. S. (1916). The laticiferous system of *Achras zapota* L. I. A preliminary account of the origin, structure, and distribution of the latex vessels in the apical meristem. *Am. J. Bot.*, **16**, 803–824.

152. KAUFMAN, P. B. and CASSELL, S. J. (1963). Striking features in the development of internodal epidermis in the oat plant (*Avena sativa*). *Mich. Bot.*, **2**, 115–121.

153. KING, N. J. and BAYLEY, S. T. (1965). A preliminary analysis of the proteins of the primary walls of some plant cells. *J. exp. Bot.*, **16**, 294–303.

154. KIRK, J. T. O. and TILNEY-BASSETT, R. A. E. (1967). *The Plastids*. Freeman, San Francisco and London.

155. KOLLMANN, R. (1964). On the fine structure of the sieve element protoplast. *Phytomorphology*, **14**, 247–264.

156. KUNDU, B. C. (1942). The anatomy of two Indian fibre plants, *Cannabis* and *Corchorus*, with special reference to the fibre distribution and development. *J. Indian bot. Soc.*, **21**, 93–128.

157. KUNDU, B. C. and SEN, S. (1961). Origin and development of fibres in ramie (*Boehmeria nivea* Gaud.). *Proc. natn. Inst. Sci. India*, B (Suppl.), **26**, 190–198.

158. LAETSCH, W. M. and STETLER, D. A. (1965). Chloroplast structure and function in cultured tobacco tissue. *Am. J. Bot.*, **52**, 798–804.

159. LAMOTTE, C. E. and JACOBS, W. P. (1962). Quantitative estimation of phloem regeneration in *Coleus* internodes. *Stain Technol.*, **37**, 63–73.

160. LAMOTTE, C. E. and JACOBS, W. P. (1963). A role of auxin in phloem regeneration in *Coleus* internodes. *Devl Biol.*, **8**, 80–98.

161. LAMPORT, D. T. A. (1965). The protein component of primary cell walls. *Adv. Bot. Res.*, **2**, 151–218.

162. LEDBETTER, M. C. and PORTER, K. R. (1963). A 'microtubule' in plant cell fine structure. *J. Cell Biol.*, **19**, 239–250.

163. LEECH, J. H., MOLLENHAUER, H. H. and WHALEY, W. G. (1963). Ultrastructural changes in the root apex. *Symp. Soc. exp. Biol.*, **17**, 74–84.

164. LEROUX, R. (1954). Recherches sur les modifications anatomiques de trois espèces d'osiers (*Salix viminalis* L., *Salix purpurea* L., *Salix fragilis* L.) provoquées par l'acide naphtalène-acétique. *C. r. Séanc. Soc. Biol.*, **148**, 284–286.

165. LIESE, W. (1965). The fine structure of bordered pits in softwoods. In *Cellular Ultrastructure of Woody Plants*, CÔTÉ, W. A., Jr., 271–290. Syracuse University Press.

166. LINSBAUER, K. (1930). *Die Epidermis. Handb. Pflanzenanat.* Band IV. Abteilung 1. Teil 2: *Histologie*. Gebrüder Borntraeger, Berlin.

167. LIVINGSTON, L. G. (1964). The nature of plasmodesmata in normal (living) plant tissues. *Am. J. Bot.*, **51**, 950–957.

168. LLOYD, F. E. (1942). *Carnivorous Plants*. Chronica Botanica, Waltham, Mass.

169. LOWARY, P. A. and AVERS, C. J. (1965). Nucleolar variation during differentiation of *Phleum* root epidermis. *Am. J. Bot.*, **52**, 199–203.

170. MACDOUGAL, D. T. (1926). Growth and permeability of century-old cells. *Am. Nat.*, **60**, 393–415.

171. MACNEISH, R. S. (1964). Ancient Mesoamerican civilization. *Science, N.Y.*, **143**, 531–537.

172. MAHLBERG, P. G. (1959a). Karyokinesis in the non-articulated laticifers of *Nerium oleander* L. *Phytomorphology*, **9**, 110–118.

173. MAHLBERG, P. G. (1959b). Development of the non-articulated laticifer in proliferated embryos of *Euphorbia marginata* Pursh. *Phytomorphology*, **9**, 156–162.

174. MAHLBERG, P. G. (1961). Embryogeny and histogenesis in *Nerium oleander*. II. Origin and development of the non-articulated laticifer. *Am. J. Bot.*, **48**, 90–99.

175. MAHLBERG, P. G. (1963). Development of non-articulated laticifer in seedling axis of *Nerium oleander*. *Bot. Gaz.*, **124**, 224–231.

176. MAHLBERG, P. G. and SABHARWAL, P. S. (1967). Mitosis in the non-articulated laticifer of *Euphorbia marginata*. *Am. J. Bot.*, **54**, 465–472.

177. MARTIN, D. J. (1955). Features on plant cuticle. An aid to the analysis of the natural diet of grazing animals, with especial reference to Scottish hill sheep. *Trans. Proc. bot. Soc. Edinb.*, **36**, 278–288.

178. METCALFE, C. R. (1967). Distribution of latex in the plant kingdom. *Econ. Bot.*, **21**, 115–127.

179. METCALFE, C. R. and CHALK, L. (1950). *Anatomy of the Dicotyledons*. Vols. I and II. Clarendon Press, Oxford.

180. MEYER, J. (1959). Le caractère précocement idioblastique des initiales stomatiques du pétiole de *Populus pyramidalis* Rozier. *Protoplasma*, **51**, 313–319.

181. MIA, A. J. and PATHAK, S. M. (1965). Histochemical studies of sclereid induction in the shoot of *Rauwolfia* species. *J. exp. Bot.*, **16**, 177–181.

182. MITCHELL, J. W. and WORLEY, J. F. (1964). Intracellular transport apparatus of phloem fibers. *Science, N. Y.*, **145**, 409–410.

183. MOLLENHAUER, H. H. and MORRÉ, D. J. (1966). Golgi apparatus and plant secretion. *A. Rev. Pl. Physiol.*, **17**, 27–46.

184. MOOR, H. (1959). Platin-Kohle-Abdrouk-Technik angewandt auf den Feinbau der milchröhren. *J. Ultrastruct. Res.*, **2**, 393–422.

185. MORRÉ, D. J., JONES, D. D. and MOLLENHAUER, H. H. (1967). Golgi apparatus mediated polysaccharide secretion by outer root cap cells of *Zea mays*. *Planta*, **74**, 286–301.

186. MORTLOCK, C. (1952). The structure and development of the hydathodes of *Ranunculus fluitans* Lam. *New Phytol.*, **51**, 129–138.

187. MÜHLETHALER, K. (1961). Plant cell walls. In *The Cell*, Vol. II, BRACHET, J. and MIRSKY, A. E., 85–134. Academic Press, New York and London.

188. MÜHLETHALER, K. (1965). Growth theories and the development of the cell wall. In *Cellular Ultrastructure of Woody Plants*, CÔTÉ, W. A., Jr., 51–60. Syracuse University Press.

189. MÜHLETHALER, K. (1967). Ultrastructure and formation of plant cell walls. *A. Rev. Pl. Physiol.*, **18**, 1–24.

190. MURMANIS, L. and EVERT, R. F. (1966). Some aspects of sieve cell ultrastructure in *Pinus strobus*. *Am. J. Bot.*, **53**, 1065–1078.

191. NEWCOMB, E. H. and BONNETT, H. T., Jr. (1965). Cytoplasmic microtubule and wall microfibril orientation in root hairs of radish. *J. Cell Biol.*, **27**, 575–589.

192. NORTHCOTE, D. H. (1963). Changes in the cell walls of plants during differentiation. *Symp. Soc. exp. Biol.*, **17**, 157–174.

193. NORTHCOTE, D. H. and PICKETT-HEAPS, J. D. (1966). A function of the Golgi apparatus in polysaccharide synthesis and transport in the root-cap cells of wheat. *Biochem. J.*, **98**, 159–167.

194. NOUGARÈDE, A. (1963). Premières observations sur l'infrastructure et sur l'évolution des cellules des jeunes ébauches foliaires embryonnaires du *Tropaeolum majus* L.: cytologie de la deshydratation de maturation. *C. r. hebd. Séanc. Acad. Sci.*, Paris, **257**, 1335–1338.

195. PALEG, L. G. (1965). Physiological effects of gibberellins. *A. Rev. Pl. Physiol.*, **16**, 291–322.

196. PANT, D. D. (1965). On the ontogeny of stomata and other homologous structures. *Plant Sci. Ser.* (*Allahabad*), **1**, 1–24.

197. PANT, D. D. and KIDWAI, P. F. (1967). Development of stomata in some Cruciferae. *Ann. Bot.*, N. S., **31**, 513–521.

198. PANT, D. D. and MEHRA, B. (1964). Ontogeny of stomata in some Ranunculaceae. *Flora, Jena*, **155**, 179–188.

199. PARTANEN, C. R. (1965). On the chromosomal basis for cellular differentiation. *Am. J. Bot.*, **52**, 204–209.

200. PEDERSEN, M. W., LE FEVRE, C. W. and WIEBE, H. H. (1958). Absorption of C^{14}-labeled sucrose by alfalfa nectaries. *Science*, N. Y., **127**, 758–759.

201. POPHAM, R. A. (1958). Some causes underlying cellular differentiation. *Ohio J. Sci.*, **58**, 347–353.

202. PORTER, K. R. (1961). The ground substance; observations from electron microscopy. In *The Cell*, Vol. II, BRACHET, J. and MIRSKY, A. E., 621–675. Academic Press, New York and London.

203. POSTLETHWAIT, S. N. and NELSON, O. E., Jr. (1957). A chronically wilted mutant of maize. *Am. J. Bot.*, **44**, 628–633.

204. REAMS, W. M., Jr. (1953). The occurrence and ontogeny of hydathodes in *Hygrophila polysperma* T. Anders. *New Phytol.*, **52**, 8–13.

205. RHODES, M. J. C. and YEMM, E. W. (1963). Development of chloroplasts and the synthesis of proteins in leaves. *Nature, Lond.*, **200**, 1077–1080.

206. ROBERTS, L. W. and FOSKET, D. E. (1962). Further experiments on wound-vessel formation in stem wounds of *Coleus. Bot. Gaz.*, **123**, 247–254.

207. ROELOFSEN, P. A. (1959). *The Plant Cell-Wall. Handb. Pflanzenanat.* Band III, Teil 4. Abteilung *Cytologie*. Gebrüder Borntraeger, Berlin.

208. ROELOFSEN, P. A. (1965). Ultrastructure of the wall in growing cells and its relation to the direction of the growth. *Adv. Bot. Res.*, **2**, 69–149.

209. ROSENE, H. F. (1954). A comparative study of the rates of water influx into the hairless epidermal surface and the root hairs of onion roots. *Physiologia Pl.*, **7**, 676–686.

210. ROTHWELL, N. V. (1964). Nucleolar size differences in the grass root epidermis. *Am. J. Bot.*, **51**, 172–179.

211. ROTHWELL, N. V. (1966). Evidence for diverse cell types in the apical region of the root epidermis of *Panicum virgatum. Am. J. Bot.*, **53**, 7–11.

212. SASSEN, M. M. A. (1965). Breakdown of the plant cell wall during the cell-fusion process. *Acta bot. neerl.*, **14**, 165–196.

213. SAX, H. J. (1938). The relation between stomata counts and chromosome number. *J. Arnold Arbor.*, **19**, 437–441.

214. SCHIEFERSTEIN, R. H. and LOOMIS, W. E. (1956). Wax deposits on leaf surfaces. *Pl. Physiol.*, Lancaster, **31**, 240–247.

215. SCHMID, R. (1965). The fine structure of pits in hardwoods. In *Cellular Ultrastructure of Woody Plants*, CÔTÉ, W. A., Jr., 291–304. Syracuse University Press.

216. SCHNEPF, E. (1960). Zur Feinstruktur der Drüsen von *Drosophyllum lusitanicum. Planta*, **54**, 641–674.

217. SCHNEPF, E. (1963a). Zur Cytologie und Physiologie pflanzlicher Drüsen. 1. Über den Fangschleim der Insektivoren. *Flora, Jena*, **153**, 1–22.

218. SCHNEPF, E. (1963b). Zur Cytologie und Physiologie pflanzlicher Drüsen. 2. Über die wirkung von Sauerstoffentzug und von Atmungsinhibitoren auf die Sekretion des Fangschleimes von *Drosophyllum* und auf die Feinstruktur der Drüsenzellen. *Flora, Jena*, **153**, 23–48.

219. SCHNEPF, E. (1965). Physiologie und Morphologie sekretarischer Pflanzenzellen. In *Sekretion und Exkretion* (2 wissenschaftliche Konferenz der Gesellschaft Deutscher Naturforscher und Ärzte, 1964), 72–88. Springer-Verlag, Berlin.

220. SCOTT, D. H. (1886). On the occurrence of articulated laticiferous vessels in *Hevea. J. Linn. Soc. (Bot.)*, **21**, 566–573.

221. SCOTT, F. M., HAMNER, K. S., BAKER, E. and BOWLER, E. (1956). Electron microscope studies of cell wall growth in the onion root. *Am. J. Bot.*, **43**, 313–324.

222. SCULTHORPE, C. D. (1967). *The Biology of Aquatic Vascular Plants.* Edward Arnold, London.

223. SIMON, S. (1908). Experimentelle Untersuchungen über die Entstehung von Gefässverbindungen. *Ber. dt. bot. Ges.*, **26**, 364–396.

224. SINNOTT, E. W. and BLOCH, R. (1939). Cell polarity and the differentiation of root hairs. *Proc. natn. Acad. Sci. U.S.A.*, **25**, 248–252.

225. SINNOTT, E. W. and BLOCH, R. (1943). Development of the fibrous net in the fruit of various races of *Luffa cylindrica. Bot. Gaz.*, **105**, 90–99.

226. SINNOTT, E. W. and BLOCH, R. (1944). Visible expression of cytoplasmic pattern in the differentiation of xylem strands. *Proc. natn. Acad. Sci. U.S.A.*, **30**, 388–392.

227. SINNOTT, E. W. and BLOCH, R. (1945). The cytoplasmic basis of intercellular patterns in vascular differentiation. *Am. J. Bot.*, **32**, 151–156.

228. SINNOTT, E. W. and BLOCH, R. (1946). Comparative differentiation in the air roots of *Monstera deliciosa. Am. J. Bot.*, **33**, 587–590.

229. SIRCAR, S. M. and CHAKRAVERTY, R. (1960). The effect of gibberellic acid on jute (*Corchorus capsularis* Linn.). *Sci. Cult.*, **26**, 141–143.

230. SJOLUND, R. D. (1968). Ultrastructural studies on tissue cultures of *Streptanthus tortuosus*. I. Differentiation of phloem elements. *Am. J. Bot.*, in press.

231. SMITH, C. EARLE, Jr. (1965). Plant fibers and civilization—cotton, a case in point. *Econ. Bot.*, **19**, 71–82.

232. SOLEREDER, H. (1908). *Systematic Anatomy of the Dicotyledons.* Clarendon Press, Oxford.

233. SOROKIN, H. P. and THIMANN, K. V. (1964). The histological basis for inhibition of axillary buds in *Pisum sativum* and the effects of auxins and kinetin on xylem development. *Protoplasma*, **59**, 326–350.

234. SOUTHORN, W. A. (1960). Complex particles in *Hevea* latex. *Nature, Lond.*, **188**, 165–166.

235. SPENCER, H. G. (1939). The effect of puncturing individual latex tubes of *Euphorbia wulfenii. Ann. Bot.*, N. S., **3**, 227–229.

236. SRIVASTAVA, L. M. (1966). On the fine structure of the cambium of *Fraxinus americana* L. *J. Cell Biol.*, **31**, 79–93.

237. STACE, C. A. (1963). *A Guide to Subcellular Botany.* Longmans, Green, London.

238. STACE, C. A. (1965). Cuticular studies as an aid to plant taxonomy. *Bull. Br. Mus. nat. Hist. (Bot.),* **4,** 1–78.

239. STAFFORD, H. A. (1948). Studies on the growth and xylary development of *Phleum pratense* seedlings in darkness and in light. *Am. J. Bot.,* **35,** 706–715.

240. STANGE, L. (1965). Plant cell differentiation. *A. Rev. Pl. Physiol.,* **16,** 119–140.

241. STANT, M. Y. (1961). The effect of gibberellic acid on fibre-cell length. *Ann. Bot., N.S.,* **25,** 453–462.

242. STANT, M. Y. (1963). The effect of gibberellic acid on cell width and the cell-wall of some phloem fibres. *Ann. Bot., N.S.,* **27,** 185–196.

243. STEBBINS, G. L. (1965). From gene to character in higher plants. *Am. Scient.,* **53,** 104–126.

244. STEBBINS, G. L. and JAIN, S. K. (1960). Developmental studies of cell differentiation in the epidermis of monocotyledons. I. *Allium, Rhoeo* and *Commelina. Devl Biol.,* **2,** 409–426.

245. STEBBINS, G. L. and KHUSH, G. S. (1961). Variation in the organization of the stomatal complex in the leaf epidermis of monocotyledons and its bearing on their phylogeny. *Am. J. Bot.,* **48,** 51–59.

246. STEBBINS, G. L. and SHAH, S. S. (1960). Developmental studies of cell differentiation in the epidermis of monocotyledons. II. Cytological features of stomatal development in the Gramineae. *Devl Biol.,* **2,** 477–500.

247. STEBBINS, G. L., SHAH, S. S., JAMIN, D. and JURA, P. (1967). Changed orientation of the mitotic spindle of stomatal guard cell divisions in *Hordeum vulgare. Am. J. Bot.,* **54,** 71–80.

248. STERLING, C. (1947). Sclereid formation in the shoot of *Pseudotsuga taxifolia. Am. J. Bot.,* **34,** 45–52.

249. STERLING, C. (1954). Sclereid development and the texture of Bartlett pears. *Fd Res.,* **19,** 433–443.

250. STEVENS, A. B. P. (1956). The structure and development of the hydathodes of *Caltha palustris* L. *New Phytol.,* **55,** 339–345.

251. STEWARD, F. C. (1963). The control of growth in plant cells. *Scient. Am.,* **209,** 104–113.

252. STEWARD, F. C. with MAPES, M. O., KENT, A. E. and HOLSTEN, R. D. (1964). Growth and development of cultured plant cells. *Science, N. Y.,* **143,** 20–27.

253. STEWARD, F. C., MAPES, M. O. and MEARS, K. (1958). Growth and organized development of cultured cells. II. Organization in cultures grown from freely suspended cells. *Am. J. Bot.,* **45,** 704–708.

254. STEWART, K. D. and CUTTER, E. G. (1967). Ultrastructure of trichoblasts and root tip cells in *Hydrocharis.* (Abstr.) *Am. J. Bot.,* **54,** 632.

255. THAINE, R. (1964). Protoplast structure in sieve tube elements. *New Phytol.,* **63,** 236–243.

256. THOMPSON, N. P. (1967). The time course of sieve tube and xylem cell regeneration and their anatomical orientation in *Coleus* stems. *Am. J. Bot.,* **54,** 588–595.

257. THOMPSON, N. P. and JACOBS, W. P. (1966). Polarity of IAA effect on sieve-tube and xylem regeneration in *Coleus* and tomato stems. *Pl. Physiol., Lancaster,* **41,** 673–682.

258. TSCHERMAK-WOESS, E. and HASITSCHKA, G. (1953). Über Musterbildung in der Rhizodermis und Exodermis bei einigen Angiospermen und einer Polypodiacee. Öst. bot. Z., 100, 646–651.

259. TSOUMIS, G. (1965). Light and electron microscopic evidence on the structure of the membrane of bordered pits in the tracheids of conifers. In Cellular Ultrastructure of Woody Plants, CÔTÉ, W. A., Jr., 305–317. Syracuse University Press.

260. TUCKER, S. C. (1964). The terminal idioblasts in Magnoliaceous leaves. Am. J. Bot., 51, 1051–1062.

261. UPHOF, J. C. TH. (1962). Plant Hairs. Handb. Pflanzenanat. Band IV, Teil 5. Abteilung: Histologie. Gebrüder Borntraeger, Berlin.

262. VARNER, J. E. and RAM CHANDRA, G. (1964). Hormonal control of enzyme synthesis in barley endosperm. Proc. natn. Acad. Sci. U.S.A., 52, 100–106.

263. VÖCHTING, H. (1878). Über Organbildung im Pflanzenreich. Max Cohen, Bonn.

264. WAISEL, Y., LIPHSCHITZ, N. and ARZEE, T. (1967). Phellogen activity in Robinia pseudacacia L. New Phytol., 66, 331–335.

265. WALKER, W. S. (1957). The effect of mechanical stimulation on the collenchyma of Apium graveolens L. Proc. Iowa Acad. Sci., 64, 177–186.

266. WALKER, W. S. (1960). The effects of mechanical stimulation and etiolation on the collenchyma of Datura stramonium. Am. J. Bot., 47, 717–724.

267. WARDROP, A. B. and HARADA, H. (1965). The formation and structure of the cell wall in fibres and tracheids. J. exp. Bot., 16, 356–371.

268. WARDROP, A. B., INGLE, H. D. and DAVIES, G. W. (1963). Nature of vestured pits in angiosperms. Nature, Lond., 197, 202–203.

269. WEIER, T. E. (1961). The ultramicro structure of starch-free chloroplasts of fully expanded leaves of Nicotiana rustica. Am. J. Bot., 48, 615–630.

270. WEIER, T. E. (1963). Changes in the fine structure of chloroplasts and mitochondria during phylogenetic and ontogenetic development. Am. J. Bot., 50, 604–611.

271. WETMORE, R. H., DEMAGGIO, A. E. and RIER, J. P. (1964). Contemporary outlook on the differentiation of vascular tissues. Phytomorphology, 14, 203–217.

272. WETMORE, R. H. and RIER, J. P. (1963). Experimental induction of vascular tissues in callus of angiosperms. Am. J. Bot., 50, 418–430.

273. WETMORE, R. H. and SOROKIN, S. (1955). On the differentiation of xylem. J. Arnold Arbor., 36, 305–317.

274. WHALEY, W. G. (1948). Rubber—the primary sources for American production. Econ. Bot., 2, 198–216.

275. WHALEY, W. G. and MOLLENHAUER, H. H. (1963). The Golgi apparatus and cell plate formation—a postulate. J. Cell Biol., 17, 216–221.

276. WHALEY, W. G., MOLLENHAUER, H. H. and LEECH, J. H. (1960). The ultrastructure of the meristematic cell. Am. J. Bot., 47, 401–448.

277. WHITAKER, D. M. (1937). Determination of polarity by centrifuging eggs of Fucus furcatus. Biol. Bull. mar. biol. Lab., Woods Hole, 73, 249–260.

278. WHITAKER, D. M. (1940). Physical factors of growth. Growth (Suppl.), (2nd Symp. Dev. Growth), 75–88.

279. WHITE, R. A. (1963). Tracheary elements of the ferns. II. Morphology of tracheary elements; conclusions. *Am. J. Bot.*, **50**, 514–522.
280. WHITMORE, T. C. (1962). Studies in systematic bark morphology. II. General features of bark construction in Dipterocarpaceae. *New Phytol.*, **61**, 208–220.
281. WHITMORE, T. C. (1963). Studies in systematic bark morphology. IV. The bark of beech, oak and sweet chestnut. *New Phytol.*, **62**, 161–169.
282. WILLIAMS, L. (1964). Laticiferous plants of economic importance. V. Resources of guttapercha—*Palaquium* species (Sapotaceae). *Econ. Bot.*, **18**, 5–26.
283. WILLIAMS, W. T. and BARBER, D. A. (1961). The functional significance of aerenchyma in plants. *Symp. Soc. exp. Biol.*, **15**, 132–144.
284. WILSON, K. (1936). The production of root-hairs in relation to the development of the piliferous layer. *Ann. Bot.*, **50**, 121–154.
285. WOODING, F. B. P. and NORTHCOTE, D. H. (1964). The development of the secondary wall of the xylem in *Acer pseudoplatanus*. *J. Cell Biol.*, **23**, 327–337.
286. WOODING, F. B. P. and NORTHCOTE, D. H. (1965a). The fine structure and development of the companion cell of the phloem of *Acer pseudoplatanus*. *J. Cell Biol.*, **24**, 117–128.
287. WOODING, F. B. P. and NORTHCOTE, D. H. (1965b). Association of the endoplasmic reticulum and the plastids in *Acer* and *Pinus*. *Am. J. Bot.*, **52**, 526–531.
288. WOODING, F. B. P. and NORTHCOTE, D. H. (1965c). The fine structure of the mature resin canal cells of *Pinus pinea*. *J. Ultrastruct. Res.*, **13**, 233–244.
289. YEMM, E. W. and WILLIS, A. J. (1954). Chlorophyll and photosynthesis in stomatal guard cells. *Nature, Lond.*, **173**, 726.
290. ZAHUR, M. S. (1959). Comparative study of secondary phloem of 423 species of woody dicotyledons belonging to 85 families. *Mem. Cornell Univ. agric. Exp. Stn*, **358**, 1–160.
291. ZIMMERMANN, M. H. (1960). Transport in the phloem. *A. Rev. Pl. Physiol.*, **11**, 167–190.
292. ZIMMERMANN, M. H. (1963). How sap moves in trees. *Scient. Am.*, **208**, 133–142.
293. ZUCKER, M. (1963). Experimental morphology of stomata. *Bull. Conn. agric. Exp. Stn*, **664**, 1–17.

INDEX

Major entries are shown in bold type, those referring to illustrations in italic type